T0050537

The Church
in the
Time of Empire

The Church
in the
Time of Empire
Resistance and Resources

David O. Woodyard

Professor of Religion
Denison University

Winchester, UK
Washington, USA

First published by Circle Books, 2011
Circle Books is an imprint of John Hunt Publishing Ltd., Laurel House, Station Approach,
Alresford, Hants, SO24 9JH, UK
office1@o-books.net
www.o-books.com

For distributor details and how to order please visit the 'Ordering' section on our website.

Text copyright: David O. Woodyard 2010

ISBN: 978-1-84694-595-3

All rights reserved. Except for brief quotations in critical articles or reviews, no part of this book may
be reproduced in any manner without prior written permission from the publishers.

The rights of David O. Woodyard as author have been asserted in accordance with the Copyright,
Designs and Patents Act 1988.

A CIP catalogue record for this book is available from the British Library.

Design: DKD

Printed in the UK by CPI Antony Rowe
Printed in the USA by Offset Paperback Mfrs, Inc

We operate a distinctive and ethical publishing philosophy in all
areas of our business, from our global network of authors to
production and worldwide distribution.

To:

Murphy Davis
and
Ed Loring

Who live the life empire fears!

CONTENTS

ACKNOWLEDGEMENTS

A college football game is an unlikely place for the beginning of a journey that climaxes in the publication of this book. The author made an offhand comment about becoming engaged with the theme of empire. David Anderson, former Provost at Denison University, replied cryptically, "Sounds like the beginning of a course" and cast his eyes back on the football field. And in the spring of 2007, it was. I am indebted to the participants in that Honors Course and their patience with an emerging interest in the Professor! They were Elyse Akhbari, Kellyann Conners, Blair Deckard, Stephanie Dixon, Courtney Herring, Elizabeth Hypes, Margaret Jaus, Ashley Jones, Stephen Julka, Ryan Linn, Tarika Mansukhani, Leslie Marshall, Anna Meeker, Abigail Miller, David Murrin-von Ebers, Kilby Pasqualone, Laura Perrings, Franklyn Steinberg.

Paul King, Professor Economics, has been my co-author in the publication of three books. (One was with Sociology / Anthropology Professor Kent Maynard.) Both have been agents of my intellectual growth in interdisciplinary studies. While Paul King has retired, I am indebted to him for a less ambitious task – critiquing this manuscript and providing sometimes painful commentary. Writing a book without his page by page participation was daunting for we have in teaching and writing developed an honest and demanding relationship. I am grateful for that, but now also for his labor on this manuscript. Obviously, I bear all the responsibility for its shortfalls.

The Union Seminary Quarterly Review has graciously permitted material that first appeared in Volume 56, 2002 to be adapted for use here.

Those who overtime have done all their professional and personal writing on time-honored "yellow pads" are a dying breed. Thankfully so, some say! There is at least one remaining Neanderthal; I am he. Therefore, the help of a person with patience, a keen eye, and a willing spirit is essential as a piece of writing emerges on a computer screen. My debt to Sandra Mead who has suffered through years of reading illegible scribbles is unmeasureable. Likely I owe her a new pair of glasses necessitated by the eye strain.

It is an honor to be able to dedicate this book to Murphy Davis and Ed Loring. They are co-founders of the OPEN DOOR COMMUNITY in Atlanta, Georgia. With a bold ministry to the homeless and victims of the prison industrial complex, they each day stare down the encroachment of empire in the lives of the defenseless. They live the faith aggressively by taking the cross off the altar and into the streets.

It has been my good fortune to spend a number of decades at Denison University. The College has provided a healthy environment for teaching, a bountiful source of support for research, and a student body of escalating excellence. President Dale T. Knobel and Provost Bradley Bateman have been friends first, able administrators, and champions of all that is excellent in the DNA of the College. Both stand tall in the profession.

FOREWARD

While some confidently think of empire apart from God, the church is the community that cannot think of God apart from empire. When the faith community functions with a radically historical tradition, it cannot bypass the context which seeks to transform and co-opt its mission... the church then and now faces conflicting claims to ultimacy, loyalty to the reign of God and the necessity of functioning in an environment empire controls. So, over time the faith community struggles with articulating the tradition while situated in a setting which either overwhelms, seeps into it, or is boldly resisted. One consequence of this is that the categories essential for God-talk are clogged by empire-talk which either prevents discourse or radically distorts it.

　　from David Woodyard, The Church in the Time of Empire, 22

The sign erected at the entrance to the long driveway of the sprawling church campus reads "Enter to Worship." Every worshiper that enters sees that sign. As worshipers leave, they view the back of that same sign, which reads "Depart to Serve." While at a first glance, this double-sided reminder is a positive way of focusing the people who come and go, the problem is that the sign leaves too much for the drivers and passengers to discern for themselves. "Worship" whom or what? "Serve" whom or what? The question is not what to do but rather the objects to which these imperatives refer. This ambiguity sums up the dilemma of present-day church and churching. We are not always aware of the gods we worship and serve.

It is hard doing church in this present culture. One of the many reasons is illumined by my colleague here in Brooklyn who argues that the church in America is becoming like the church in Europe: As society becomes increasingly secular, the church will be rendered irrelevant. He makes a strong point, but I argue that it is not secularity that holds the church hostage. Rather, it is the particular type of religion – and I mean here principally the type of Christianity – that we espouse and practice. It is a religion that is subsumed in and pays homage to the "divinity" of our brand of democracy and the allegiance to our specific brand of capitalism that has effectively transformed many local churches into the promoters and consumers of an ideology that falls short of true worship and service. These "peddlers of the word" display their goods with great polish and effectiveness, and the church cannot separate the American idea and dream from the worship of God who was in Christ Jesus. For example, it's the seventh inning stretch at many major league ballparks where "Take Me Out to the Ball Game" has been replaced with "God Bless America." To be a good Christian is to be a good American, and that, quite frankly, is very dangerous.

These are not new times for the Christian church. It has always been a challenge for faithful Christians to strike a balance between a healthy participation in society as salt and light while at the same time resisting the temptation to make gods of one's life, lifestyle, culture or political position. However, to make god of any of these things is to do injury to the divine decree "have no other gods before me."

There are times in a nation's history where the trespass into the sacred is glaring and undeniable. There are other times, like the one in which we presently live, where we find it hard to distinguish and draw the line between these areas. The subtle and sometimes subliminal message preached underneath the gospel Sunday to Sunday is "serve the empire with gladness." *The Church in the Time of Empire* surfaces and subverts this.

One of the challenges for those of us who still believe in the efficacy of sacred community, is that we have become dulled, bored and boring by practicing rituals and performing rhetoric that offer no opportunity for our congregations to engage in practices of resistance that offer alternative narratives to empire. For example, what does the rite of baptism mean except that we are initiated into a new holy configuration of God's reign called by many of us now "the kin-dom of God." This intentional framing of God's reign as kin-dom resists being confused with empire because it refuses to speak of God's sovereign relationship "over us" and stresses the profound sense of belonging and kinship to be felt by all who are joyous participants in it.

In our church, we serve communion once a month with the small individual communion cups. The way that we serve could be another reinforcement of the callous myopia that marks much of "sacred practice" performed in contemporary churches. However, before the officers return from serving the people at their seats, we pause to ask if anyone has been overlooked, and we refuse to eat or drink until all have been served. This is our commitment as practicing Christians: We will not eat until everyone is served. What happens if this simple ritual is translated into action outside the church walls? What if we understand radically that "remembrance of Christ" is making sure that all have been served equally? What happens when a church profoundly moved by this sacred act of inclusion realizes that it cannot truly rest until all in the world are fed? What a glaring contrast to the works of empire that, by necessity, has some who must go first, some who must be last, and some who are ignored even though they are forced to go without! *The Church in the Time of Empire* affords us the significant opportunity to begin questioning the defining dynamics of progressive Christian practices.

When our hymns, songs, prayers and sermons fail to envision and inspire us to do justice, love mercy and walk humbly with God, our entrances and exits from houses of worship do no more than perpetuate the kinds of societal and systemic ways in which we remain chained to a worship of ourselves, broken and fragmented as we are.

Gary V. Simpson, Senior Pastor
The Concord Baptist Church of Christ
Brooklyn, New York
8 November 2010

THE CONTOURS
OF EMPIRE

CHAPTER ONE

Introduction

Americans recoil from thinking of our nation as an empire; unless, of course, it is seen as a benevolent designation. Patriotism is a bulwark against imagining ourselves as having a dubious role in history. While we are able to think of another country as an "evil empire," what Shriver calls our "civic pride" stands in the way of "civic shame" when we reflect on America.[1] The ambiguity that should result from entertaining both does not readily enter in our consciousness. Randall Robinson calls attention to an historic irony: "To erect the building that would house the art that symbolized American democracy, the United State government sent out a request for a hundred slaves ... In exchange for the slaves' labor the government agreed to pay their *owners* five dollars per month per slave."[2] If nothing else, that is a metaphor for our national duplicity. Our most noble aspiration may be contradicted by our actions. And it is this same contradiction that creates a consciousness that resists the implication we are an empire. National innocence dominates our national self-identity; and it is a basic immunization against reality.

The existing literature on empire, and America as an empire, vastly exceeds the appearances of the term in public discourse. Occasionally it emerges in the form of a denial, or in reference to the past. It is seldom referential in identifying our current or past national actions or self-perception. Perhaps the instances of empire are so abundant Americans don't think of gathering them in a category! But consider some of the books published in the last decade or so by authors in a wide range of disciplines and life experiences. The titles alone reveal consequential reflection on our national life. *Among*

Empires: American Ascendency and Its Predecessors (Charles S. Maier, Professor of History). *American Empire: The Realities and Consequences of U.S. Diplomacy* (Andrew J. Bacevich, Professor of International Relations). *America's Inadvertent Empire* (William E. Odam, Retired Army General and Robert Dujarric, Professor of Political Science). *The Sorrows of Empire: Militarism, Secrecy, and the End of the Republic* (Chalmers A. Johnson, President of a Policy Institute). *Christians in the American Empire: Faith and Citizenship in the New World Order* (Vincent D. Rougeau, Professor of Law). *God and Empire: Jesus Against Rome, Then and Now* (John Dominic Crossan, Professor of New Testament). *Empire and the Christian Tradition* (Kwok Pui-Lan, et al, Professors of Theology). Empire may not be on the radar of Americans but those who focus on the phenomenon and America as an empire are legion. And its seepage into public discourse may be inevitable, however reluctant.

The disconnect between the public discourse and professional reflection may be accounted for, in part, by the mask of humanitarianism. By extending our jurisdiction globally we were and are just doing good. Timothy H. Parsons notes that "...such humanitarianism rests on the premise that nonwestern people were in need of salvation."[3] And for Parsons "salvation" is secular in nature; we save them from themselves and their more base instincts! He goes on to claim boldly, "Empire has never been more than naked self-interest."[4] That is hardly an attractive identity for America to claim.

On a Sunday morning it would be unusual for the worshipers to hear a reference to empire; certainly, the seepage of empire into the church's consciousness is unexamined. The same silence also forfeits a consideration of the churches responsibility in relation to empire. Given the tension in the biblical record between the faith communities and empire, the contemporary default is particularly egregious. It is not sufficient to explain this by the recognition the private and personal sphere has been the voice to which religious tradition has responded. The more telling default is the degree to which issues are addressed in the public sphere without a recognition they are often driven by the demands of empire. Hunger and poverty can be referenced and addressed without discerning the role the economy as an agent of empire has in creating the condition. We will address this in a later chapter. To think of hunger and poverty as isolated from empire is to ignore the roots of the problem in the economic system.

The issues of empire are ones of institutional power. To redress those issues calls for institutional counter power. If the church takes the biblical tradition seriously, it will be called to act as an agent of resistance. The church is not the only institution for contesting misuse of power, but it is one with the longest history in America!

Empire Defined, Endorsed, and Critiqued

Surfacing a more complete definition of empire is an appropriate starting point. Intuitively empire seems to be something anchored in the distant past and without evident contemporary contours. Hardt and Negri sharpen and focus our understanding. "The concept of empire is characterized fundamentally by a lack of boundaries. Empire's rule has no limits."[5] An empire exists when one nation aspires to control the reality in which other nations exist. In the crudest sense it is a posture of "norm-setting." A former and Democratic Secretary of State claimed that America is "the indispensible nation."[6] As such it has the right and responsibility to impose its values and institutions on the world – and totally subordinate the interests of others. The obvious and not so subtle goal for an indispensible nation is "by any means necessary" to force other nations to correspond to our sense of reality. What is normal for us, and therefore right, deserves to be imposed on others. To be more specific, an empire exists when one nation unilaterally assumes global jurisdiction; when it marshals the power to define the social, political, and economic texture of other nations; when an elite within one nation is able to make its interests controlling.

While Americans may not immediately identify our nation with those roles, consider this. An empire exists when the economic system of one nation through a transnational corporation controls what a farmer in Brazil can earn for coffee beans. An empire exists when one nation engages in "a decade of unprecedented interventionalism"[7] with violent engagements in Bosnia, Haiti, Kosovo, Afghanistan, and Iraq to name a few. An empire exists when one nation assumes that its vision of freedom should be imposed "by any means necessary" on nations whose peoples and institutions are not attuned to it. An empire exists when one nation claims to be authorized by God to assert itself into the culture of another nation and void its values and institutions. An empire exists when a nation sets an agenda "to rid the world of evil" (G. W. Bush) and assume the right to dominate and define where evil exists. In the words of Pogo, "We have met the enemy, and it is us." National arrogance is evident and deification as well. That may be why President Bush, while acting as "emperor-in-chief," was quick to deny we are an empire.

We should not be deluded by the fact that at times we may be "right." The issue is what gives us this "right" to impose our will. Power is an excuse, not an authorization! "Exceptionalism" is often used to support this use of power. It is the heart-beat of our life as empire. Often theological legitimation follows. One of our sacred texts is a sermon preached by John Winthrop allegedly, on board the Arabella as the ship was departing the new land in 1630. Some contend it was actually delivered in a church sometime before their departure. The imagery that is invoked to support the unique role of America in the world is: "Wee shall be as a Citty upon a Hill, the eies of all people are upon us; ..." Recent Presidents (Reagan, Johnson, and Bush) among others see these words as pivotal in articulating exceptionalism. "Citty upon a Hill" represents privilege and innocence and the right to serve as a compelling model for others. And the hidden clause often includes the right to impose our excellence. What is neglected is the beginning of the paragraph which defines the imagined agenda. It calls up the words of Micah and then "For this end, wee must be knitt together in this worke as one man, wee must entertain each other in brotherly Affeccion, wee must be willing to abridge our selves of our superfluities, for the supply of others necessities, wee must uphold a familiar Commerce together in all meekness, gentlenes, patience and liberality, wee must delight in each other, make others Condicions our owne, ... as members of the same body, ... (and) keepe the unitie of the spirit in the bond of peace..."[8] The sense of aspiration invoked by those words collapses into fulfillment when "as a Citty upon a Hill" is taken as existent. And what follows is missionary energy joined with the power to prevail.

Exceptionalism assumes unique gifts which have been actualized and the right to impose them (some say offer) on others. Apparently purity is not compromised by power but advanced by it. And what underwrites this exceptionalism is a contract with God which America executes. Harkening back to John Winthrop's sermon for authorization, the high priests of nationalism claim we are "God's New Israel" and a "chosen people" and therefore have a distinct destiny to bring others into line with our values and institutions. Preemptive action is not only an option but an obligation. While denying the designation of America as an empire, President Bush "preached," "America is a nation with a mission ... The liberty we prize is not America's gift to the world. It is God's gift to the world... (There) is a wonder-working power in the goodness and idealism and faith of the American people." In short, we can do what we are doing because God is behind us. Exceptionalism is endorsed by the Almighty and we are but servants of God's purposes. Fortunately, who we are is not modified by ambiguity.

The irony in most who invoke "the Citty on a Hill" imagery is that they de-contextualize it. They treat it as a description not an aspiration. We forget that "Winthrop was not an American ... he was an Englishman ...whose religious beliefs put him at odds with the contemporary government of King Charles I and his domineering archbishop of Canterbury, William Laud." The sermon had to do with imagining a colony radically different from the one he inhabited.

"... he could not have therefore imagined that the United Stated would be as a city upon a hill ... he was preaching to Englishmen"[9] about the need for an alternative. There is no valid linkage between the sermon by Winthrop and the uses of it by Presidents Reagan and Bush. This is not a birth but an abortion. Yet exceptionalism is a dominant theme in our self-description and self-legitimation. And if one aspires to be theological, one might say it assumes America as a nation escaped the Fall; somehow pervasive self-interest was bypassed. Thus we have a right and obligation to spread our unique gifts, confident that we embody them and it is our destiny.

While we have problematized exceptionalism, there are many beyond public figures that make a virtue of it. The "Project for the New American Century" is an exquisite example. The PNAC broadens the boundaries of exceptionalism and celebrates the outer limits of the concept.

Founded in 1997, the PNAC defines itself as an educational endeavor "whose goal is to provide American global leadership." Recognizing that our nation is "the world's most preeminent power," it has an obligation and "resolve to shape a new century favorable to American principles and interests." Given a military that is "strong and ready," it is called to global leadership. The goal is "to shape circumstances before crises emerge, and to meet threats before they become dire."[10] The project is not restrained or encumbered by ambiguity. The world needs order and America has the gifts and the capabilities to enforce it. Absent a global rival, its mission is both noble, achievable, and necessary. The emergence of a rival is not only unnecessary but to be prevented "by any means necessary."

The centerpiece of the PNAC is articulated in the document, "Rebuilding America's Defenses." Weakness or humility has no role in world governance. Strategy has to be substantiated by resources. America's privileged position cannot be taken for granted but nourished by a restored and reconstituted military which "should aim to preserve and extend this advantageous position as far into the future as possible." At present, the military is "undermanned, inadequately equipped and trained, ... and ill-prepared to handle contingency operations..."[11] Only a newly financed and disciplined focus can serve "geopolitical ends" which America is uniquely qualified to establish. Mission requires might; peace is created by power relationships.

"Pax Americana" is the goal, a peace and world order that serves the interests of all. That benign image would seem to mask the unilateralism and domination which are agents of the agenda. The structuring of forces into an emerging order where America's interests match those of all is justified by the end in view. Power and peace are coordinates. Our moral clarity equips us to accomplish our goals in the interests of all by the threat or use of violence. Our use of power to bring peace and freedom is both logical and just.

Michael Mandelbaum is an articulate dissenter from the claim America functions in the world as an empire. While he wants to exorcise the language of empire from our verbal DNA, he reclaims much of what it designates. World conditions require a role to which America has laid claim. However, our presence in the world is benign, even noble. He claims, "The United States ....functions as the world's government."[12] While acknowledging that there is power in that role, it is on behalf of the interests of world order. We are needed; we are "a provider of services for society"[13] without which there would be chaos. And our services are not driven by narrow forms of self-interest as we create global stability. Our role is to provide the security necessary for global peace and prosperity. We are not encumbered by "naked self-interest."

Mandelbaum argues his case in two directions. One is the recognition that empire has three characterizations, none of which match our performance. The first is "subordination," the existence of unequal relationships. Other nations are partners not victims in seeking a just world order. A second is "coercion," the reality of threat and resort to force; that is not in our arsenal. Our efforts for world government are benign. Finally, empire is "a form of dictatorship ...

by foreigners external control."[14] Trusteeship is our style and global domination is not an aspiration. America escapes these features as it assumes the role that steers the world order in the interests of all. That leads into the second support for his position. We are not only present in history with the will and capacity to serve but there is "a broad and unprecedented consensus" about what is needed and of which we are exemplar. Mandelbaum describes these as, "...peace as the optimal condition of international relations and the proper aim of foreign policy; democracy as the best form of government; and the free market as the only satisfactory way of organizing economic affairs."[15] The confluence of our values and institutions and our ability to share them effectively constitute the good fortune of the 21st century. Everyone benefits. Without us, disorder would reign. Who we are and what we can do converge in ways that might be seen as a secular providence. The war in Iraq might serve to problematize that claim.

Exceptionalism and the Iraq War

While we have been exploring America as an empire, an issue becomes whether exceptionalism is a vice or a virtue. One of the ways to examine that tension would be to consider the Iraq war as an expression of exceptionalism. Was it, is it, an example of global statesmanship or egregious dominance and intervention grounded in a determination to shape the Middle East according to our interests? Some would contend that its origins in 9/11 gave empire aspirations a new inteinsty.

The case for prudent statesmanship is made by the PNAC document, "Iraq: Setting the Record Straight" published in April 2005.[16] By that date the issue of weapons of mass destruction had been shelved. But the threat had been imbedded in the national consciousness and hovered in the background. One does not readily expunge from consciousness the words of Secretary of Defense Donald Rumsfeld on "Face the Nation" September 2, 2002. He asked, "Imagine a September eleventh with weapons of mass destruction.

It is not three thousand – its tens of thousands of innocent men, women and children."[17] This does not necessarily mean that the threat is imminent, that an attack is likely in the near future. The PNAC document talks about the present as an opportunity to act before the consequences are dire. Saddam has a history that is foreboding in the least. "The history of Saddam's regime was well known: war against Iran; war against Kuwait; war against Iraqis; mass murder and mass graves; poison gas attacks; ethnic cleansing; institutionalized torture and repression; aiding terrorist organization; ..."[18] Regional domination clearly is his agenda, and at any price.

According to the PNAC document, the time is ripe for acting on behalf of global interests; the cause is just and we alone have the power to intervene. In a sense, we were created for such a time as this. The good of all will be preserved by military intervention. Global statesmanship and military might merge to manage the peace and stability of the Middle East. That this is an example of exceptionalism at its best is reflected in the claim by President Bush the attack was a selfless act by a great nation.

It is important to note the intimate linkage between public figures and the documents on defense of the PNAC. The signatures include eighteen persons who were well-placed in the administration, ten in prominent positions. Consider several: Vice President Dick Cheney; Secretary of Defense Donald Rumsfeld, Secretary of State Colin Powel, with Jed Bush as relational intimate. Key figures in the administration were certainly positioned to influence policy, even define it. PNAC's ideology was in power.

While this event can be used to legitimate exceptionalism, it also masks its presumption and demonic potential. Certainly one issue that can be raised is that of unambiguous righteousness. Does any nation, system, or institution embody such moral clarity that its right to rule is inherently legitimate? Is it possible that any nation is exempt from sin – or consuming self-interest in secular terms? Or does a will to power conceal itself as virtue? This leads to the question if might leads to right; because you can you should? When benevolence and military might become fused, capacity gets confused with necessity. Add a dose of messianism and presumed generosity and power corrupts the moral clarity. There is also the issue of what is neglected when violence is the means to peace and events are constructed in the ideology of good and evil. Nelson-Pallmeyer quotes an observation of Amnesty International; "…they have allowed the real weapons of mass destruction – injustice and impurity, poverty, discrimination and race, the uncontrolled trade in small areas, violence against women and abuse of children – to go unaddressed."[19] Exceptionalism becomes, then, a detour from the very values and traditions which have defined the American reality.

We have been contending that empire in the form of exceptionalism is at play in the Iraq war. Even those who resist the language of empire, even empire-lite, embrace exceptionalism as operational in America's foreign policy. One issue we have not explicitly explored is the theological spin to exceptionalism. It is prominent in the sermon by Winthrop, well beyond invoking the passage from Micah. In describing the vision and mission he imagines, Winthrop assures the people (either congregation or shipmates) that "wee shall finde that the God of Israell is among us…"[20] The preacher is overlaying the exodus event on the search for a new world which will be 'a Citty upon a Hill," casting its light over others and inviting them to model themselves (or be modeled over) what would become America. For Winthrop, exceptionalism is God's way of working in the world, even as God led the Israelites to a promised world. When we transition from the 1600's to the 21st century, President Bush does not hesitate to identify military actions as the centerpiece of "a divinely sanctioned crusade against evil."[21] We have been called as a "chosen people" to engage evil and rid the world of it with whatever it takes in the way of military initiatives. Ironically, Bush and bin Laden have one thing in common and that is a commitment to a holy war! For our part, divine providence now controls America's foreign policy and the President has become a savior (with bombs and troops). God acts unilaterally and violently! In remarks to the nation after 9/11, President Bush began his theological journey with the claim, "God is not neutral." And God has an agent, perhaps a Moses, in the White House.

Exceptionalism has now taken the form of claiming, God knows what God is doing and we are God's willing servants. That sounds more like empire than global statesmanship!

When Michael Mandelbaum contends it is "inaccurate" to designate America as an empire, he draws upon a definition of it by Michael Doyle: empires are "relationships of political control imposed by some political societies over the effective sovereignty of other societies."[22] And, as noted earlier, there are three features of empire, none of which are evident in America. They are subordination, coercion, and dictatorship by foreigners. When Mandelbaum identifies what America is really doing in the world he claims, "America acts as the world's government."[23] And he distinguishes between a government and an empire by claiming the first "steers" and the second "commands." Governments lead while empires impose. In a sense, governments are noble while empires are self-serving. The one is benign while the other is devious.

If, as we have argued, empire has as its central doctrine exceptionalism, and the Iraq war is a manifestation of it, then we have the data with which to explore the three criteria in relation to America's way of being in the world. Given our analysis, there can be little doubt about the conclusion of being an empire. However, the three criteria cut in the opposite direction from what Mandelbaum contends. First, when subordination is understood as "unequal relationship," clearly a world power is intervening in the political, economic, and social relationship of a smaller nation. And the attempt to draw into an invasion representative forces of other nations only compounds the inequity. Mandelbaum may think of America as "Goliath" but that very image undermines his position. Second, "coercion" is evident in the very act of bombing another country, deposing its leader, and occupying it in some measure. Bombs are more like commanding than steering! Third, "dictatorship by foreigners" is clearly evident in the act of bringing democracy to the Middle East as President Bush so frequently affirmed. In the measure America aspires to impose its political and economic order on Iraq, that would seem an obvious form of "dictatorship by foreigners."

While there is something eloquent about the book by Mandelbaum, what is "inaccurate" is his contention. His criteria for judging cut in the opposite direction and establishes America as an empire.

Empire as Religion

In the introduction to this chapter, we claimed the church has a responsibility and obligation to be a community of resistance to empire. In later chapters we will establish that this role is authorized by the biblical tradition and sustained by the practice of worship. Here we compound that role with attending to several issues on which the church is uniquely qualified to "call out" the fact of America as an empire.

There are places in our text where we acknowledge that some persons are religious about empire. President Bush declares we are not an empire but then proceeds to give a religious spin to our acting like one. He has no doubt that in "steering" events in the Middle East by violence we are doing God's will and acting on God's behalf. What we have not considered is the possibility that others in a secular framework see empire functioning as a religion – whether or not they would use that language. There are several ways in which one can support the argument that empire is a religion, perhaps faintly disguised.

One of the ways in which to support that contention is to discover empire has unnamed god concepts. There are masked god concepts in apparently godless settings and ideology. Empire has assumptions which are authoritive, almighty, and atomistic. Traditional divine qualities get transferred from a deity to an empire. Douglas Meeks in another context notes that for some "God chooses, elects, and determines according to an atomistic sovereignty."[24] Hence, God is a transcendent entity who authorizes the conditions of existence and rationalizes relationships, all within an absolutist and perfectionist nature. There is often a streak of domination in God concepts and it is expressed in images like king, omniscient, even omnipotent. And that does not even consider the role of Creator or providential activity.

When we think of America's role as empire (and at times the President as emperor), the qualities of god concepts are clearly at play. Empire is transcendent in that it is beyond and not subject to ambiguity. It may not have an immaculate conception but functions as if it did. Empire is creator in that it claims the right and obligation to define relationships and order the conditions for others. Reality has its origin in empire. Empire is omniscient in that its assumptions and actions are not subject to dispute (at least from within!). It knows the truth and it represents it without a sense of ambiguity, or modesty. Empire is omnipotent, not only in the sense it has the resources but the power to impose and the will to do so. When a nation is the one superpower with the determination to defeat rivals, nothing constrains force. And, empire is self-sufficient and singular with purity of purpose and inordinate capabilities to impose its exceptional qualities on others. In summary, then, there are god concepts imbedded in empire which are functioning as America assumes the role that some might think of as statesmanship. You do not have to be a god to function like one!

When Reinhold Niebuhr wrote in 1959 about empire, he argued that one of the characteristic motives for "extension of domain" is essentially missionary in nature. It is driven by "the conviction that the imperial power either represents a universal community or that it is able to bestow a value of universal validity."[25] The presumption is that our nation has the right values, principles, and institutions and therefore is obligated to share them – often by any means necessary! The reality of missionary zeal is rooted in the confidence that the empire exemplifies what is best for others and generously (often forcefully!) makes it available to them. If you have the truth, even embody it, some religious commitment drives the willingness to create a world that thrives on it. If a nation's political, social, economic order are right for the world then a passionate determination to share them is a moral duty. Cultural imposition is a right and a necessity. Empires do that and it is evidence of a secular religion, functioning like one.

Another characteristic of religion evident in empire is a kind of secular providence. Empires have a necessary – and they think legitimate - ordering function, the creation of a new world order. We noted above that George Bush identified the action of God with the action of America. But there is a 'godless" religion in empire that functions much like "the invisible hand" in Adam Smith; something is working its way through events and it happens to have America at the rudder. President Bush may have aspired to appeal to secularists when he spoke of "a wonder working power" in history which happens to be active in us. What takes the place of "the kingdom of God" is a kind of utopianism uncontaminated by modesty. Reinhold Niebuhr refers to "collective security" which is the means of preserving and advancing this utopia.[26] And it is predicated on the conviction there is a world to be where America's principal values, and institutions can define reality for a global community. Apparently there are no limits to human striving as long as security is the goal. Empire can pursue that state with self-assurance and with force if necessary. In May 1930 in "The Atlantic Monthly" Niebuhr wrote of Americans as "awkward imperialists." If writing in the 21st century, "awkward" might have to be reconsidered. With a secular providence apparent, empire no longer needs to be self-conscious or subject to doubt about the ends or the means of the goal or security. The watch for terrorist trumped any scruples about means or ambiguity about ends. An empire has the right to do what it has to in pursuit of a new order of freedom.

This goal of empire sounds strangely like "the Kingdom of God on earth," albeit without a moral core of restraint. While our "reach is beyond our grasp," responsibility for reaching is limitless and the goal is marked by moral clarity. Empire is more religious than some religions when it comes to providential action in the global sphere. The "invisible hand" is evident and effective.

Empire is a religion, a secular one at least, and its ultimacy is beyond question. Critique is unpatriotic. Prophets are without honor. But the church as a counter institution has a calling it cannot forfeit without negating its heritage in the biblical tradition.

While some may be in denial, the reality is that America is an empire. It may appear to be in the role of world government or statesmanship, but it is statesmanship and government with nuclear weapons. That alone collapses "steering" into "commanding."

EMPIRE AND TRANSCENDENCE

CHAPTER TWO

Introduction

While some confidently think of empire apart from God, the church is the community that cannot think of God apart from empire. When the faith community functions with a radically historical tradition, it cannot bypass the context which seeks to transform and co-opt its mission. Our study of Scripture in the next Chapter will surface the reality that the early church consistently positioned itself in resistance to empire, sometimes more successfully than others. The Gospels stand as evidence that Jesus lived in an occupied country, even as we do today. As such, the church then and now faces conflicting claims to ultimacy, loyalty to the reign of God and the necessity of functioning in an environment empire controls. So, over time the faith community struggles with articulating the tradition while situated in a setting which either overwhelms, seeps into it, or is boldly resisted. One consequence of this is that the categories essential for God-talk are clogged by empire-talk which either prevents discourse or radically distorts it.

The Subversion of Discourse

In the last chapter we considered the hidden or implicit God concepts in the ideology of empire. The presumption of godlessness was unmasked. God-concepts are mysteriously imbedded in a posture perceived to be totally immanental, within history. Now we aspire to reverse the agenda and ask, "How does empire subvert and distort the thought categories essential for the articulation of transcendence?" Empire is driven by an ideology that aspires to disconfirm the environment in which God language is formulated. The dark side of empire for the church is that it preempts the linguistic landscape in which the presence of transcendence is negotiated. Empire itself becomes transcendent. As such, it is pre-emptive and disruptive. We will consider three examples.

One of the categories "captured" by empire is that of power. Empire and power are almost interchangeable terms; they are virtually synonymous. And there is nothing seen as problematic about either of them. Within the context of empire power is perceived to be inherently good and absolute; empire has power along with a legitimate claim to define reality for others with it. The transactions of empire are essentially power-driven, and confidently so. Power is the "weapon of choice," necessity as well. Domination of the public sphere is legitimate and obligatory in achieving the goals of empire. And it is the power to overpower, to control, and to stipulate in the world order.

In the service of empire, power has many facets or forms. John Dominic Crossan referencing Michael Mann[1] notes that "social power" is a coalition of multiple forms of power which work in consort to achieve the goals of empire. There is "military power, the monopoly or control by force and violence; economic power, the monopoly or control of labor; political power, the monopoly or control of organization and institution; and ideological power, the monopoly or control of the interpretation of meaning." Crossan identifies how each of these was manifest in the Roman Empire. And he unmasks the four fold forms of power in the events of 9/11; "social power" in collusion is evident there.[2] The Pentagon struck by A.A. flight 77 symbolized military power. The target was not incidental! The Twin Towers of the World Trade Center struck by A.A. flight 11 and U.A. flight 175 surface economic power - no incidental objects. The White House was evidently the goal of U.A. flight 93 (intercepted from hitting by courageous passengers) as a statement about political power. And the ways in which the interpreting and meaning of the events were controlled is the work of ideological power. As a consequence terrorists were successful in drawing us into a response against Iraq. The public was disposed to ask, "Why do they hate us?" That only personalized the issue; of course, for direct victims and their families it was intensely personal. While in 9/11 the American people were victims, they were not the intended target. For the terrorists the "us" is empire and the forms of power which dominated the globe, or aspires to. One does not have to be a pacifist to recognize the reality of corruption in power evident in these events.

The assumption of empire is that power is innocent and necessary. It is also absolute. And it is the handmaiden of empire.

Power is also implicated in God-talk. But when power has been defined by empire, the ability of the faith community to talk about omnipotence, providence, and the Kingdom of God is imperiled. While there are instances when power has been tainted by a sense of "overpowered," that is not an authentic representation of the faith tradition. Rather, theologically the task is to relate God to history and persons within it in more relational and mutual terminology. Restraint of power is a more characteristic mode of God's being. Paul even talks about the power of weakness. He contends we should "Welcome one another..." and risk vulnerability (Romans 14:7). While the Gospel "is the power of God for salvation to everyone who has faith" (Romans 1:16) our faith is a condition of the power's prevailing. While "God works for good (it is) with those who love him" (Romans 8:28) and not random prevailing. And when we turn to I Corinthians 1:25-26, we hear that the "weakness of God" is the mode of relationship in partnership with the claim, "God chooses what is weak in the world." In no sense is the biblical God "a unilateral superpower"[3] but one who lures creation out of chaos and leads rather than drives the Israelites to a promised land. In no sense is there overpowering or determined outcomes.

When empire controls the meaning of power and represents it as innocent, necessary, and absolute, that clogs the discourse on theological turf and resists the understanding of the modes of God's acting in history. There the worship of power yields the powerlessness of a tradition.

Second, when empire controls the discourse, there is no place for ambiguity; indeed, it is rigorously precluded. Rather, there are binary constructions. Reality is constructed in terms of good vs. evil; empire is good and anything at odds with it is demonized. Dissent is unpatriotic! In the last chapter we explored American exceptionalism. It is the claim that our sense of reality – politically, socially, and economically – is so pure and true that we are obligated to impose it on others. What is good for us is good for every nation – whether they want it or not. There is no attention to context as it might influence events and reciprocity is not an option. The transactions of empire in every sphere are unambiguous.

As American empire with a firm grasp on exceptionalism, the rationale for existence becomes exporting reality. The presumption is that other national entities are socially, politically, and economically deprived and even depraved. Nothing really is as it should be – by our standards. And what we have to offer is pure as well as innocent. Nothing elsewhere is significant, worthy of value, or emulatable. In a sense, the "other" is made up of non-persons, non-places, and for non-purposes. Their institutions, systems, and values call out for displacement. The earlier consideration of the Iraq war is a case in point. President Bush was called by God to bomb that nation as a means of establishing there what is valued and embodied here. The God factor legitimates the exporting and renders it unambiguously good. Some would say it was a noble as well as necessary invasion. Absent the category of ambiguity, the possible becomes necessary.

Sociologist George Ritzer writes about this phenomenon as "Americanization." It is more than a growth of influence. Rather, it is "the propagation of American ideas, customs, social patterns, industry, and capital around the world."[4] As such, it is unidirectional and void of complexities. At every level it is cultural imperialism allegedly in the interests of all. It is not a hybrid act toward blending, bad as that would be, but an act of saturation without regard for cultural victims. The presumption is that what is local is deficient at best and dysfunctional at worst. Ritzer identified the "consumption model" as one form of Americanization. [5] Systems of advertising and marketing overwhelm whatever is local. Have you even been in another country with no McDonald's restaurants or Coke advertisements? Ritzer notes, "American exporters...conceal the roots of these exports and transforms them into ever-emptier forms that can adapt to virtually any locale."[6] He might better have said, overwhelming a locale. And all of this without any sense of ambiguity.

It might not be immediately evident why God-talk requires a clear sense of ambiguity. Some would associate it with the unambiguous; isn't God perfect? But think of Reinhold Niebuhr, and even his brother H. Richard. The Christian message, and hence God-talk, never fits in this world but hovers over it in sketchy discourse. And the Reign of God is never embodied even as it is historized. God-talk is always at the "edges of language" and God's action is always identified with humility and tentativeness. The identification of divinity and the designation of its activity never go beyond problematic designation. This is not to ignore the presence of those who name the work of God and identity it uniquely with America and their personal lives as well; but they violate the nature of transcendence in the process. There is a proverb that suggests a God defined is a God denied. When ambiguity has been liquidated authentic God-talk has been marginalized.

The unambiguous reach of empire clogs the category in which language of transcendence is negotiated.

A third category distorted by empire is that of agency. Agency concerns the ways in which a principle acts in relation to another, in this instance between nations. Inevitably some degree of power is present in the transaction. But the central issue is the nature of the activity and how one nation regards another. Does the agent enhance, dignify, and respect the other or commodity the recipient of the activity? Is the agency enabling or diminishing? What is the quality of the interaction between social bodies? Is it enabling or disabling? Is the one acted upon treated as a subject or an object?

Empire is destructive of the process of agency. The transactions are consistently ones which are marked by "othering." They objectify and exploit for their own purposes. In the imagery of Martin Buber (in the personal realm) they are "I-It" interactions rather than "I-Thou" ones. Empire acts without any reciprocity or risk of response. Because empire has the power and is not restrained by ambiguity, it imposes reality; the other nation is simply an entity to be molded – "by any means necessary." Much in the manner some missionaries aspired to convert the heathen without regard for their culture or traditions, empire aspires to remake the world after its images of social, political, and economic reality. Grounded in exceptionalism, empire's mission is demonization of what it finds and transformation into the agents' sense of good and true. Godfrey Hodgson refers to this as "missionary exceptionalism... the belief that it is the destiny, some say God-given destiny, of the United States to spread the benefits of its democratic system and of its specific version of capitalism to as many other countries as possible." [7] That happens to be a conspicuously undemocratic form of agency! Again, as President Bush said, "we have a calling from beyond the stars to stand for freedom... Now we go forward ... faithful to our cause and confident in the future of the greatest nation on earth."[8] At every level, what is "there" is trivialized and subject to reconstruction in our image. The nature of American agency is one of domination and desecration. The empire operates in the mode of "hegemonic unipolarity."[9] Here the distinction emerges between an empire and a republic. The agency of a republic is participatory and seeks the well-being of all, by their consent. An empire's mode of agency is unambiguous action in pursuit of replication of what we have seen as "right" and embodied in our national existence. Agency in empire is unilateral and linear, and finally serves its own interests, often under the guise of altruism. Empire's agency diminishes and distorts the "other," the recipient of its imposition. In all realms it is virtually impossible to "escape its force field completely."[10]   In empire the transactions are imperialistic.

When agency is conceived and executed by empire it resists the reality of transcendence necessary for the biblical God. While agency is unilateral and linear in empire it is relational for God-talk. God's agency is not only void of needs but advances and enables the recipient. And while it cherishes human selfhood, it provokes solidarity with others. Agency in the empire overwhelms while agency in God-talk results in solicitude. The interests of the self are inseparable from those of others. Rather than lead to domination, God's agency creates community within which selfhood is nurtured and shared. At this point it is common to invoke the Trinity as representative of God's being and the well-being of others. The three persons are distinguishable but inseparable. And relationality provokes relationality. What it means, then, to be involved in God-talk is to engage in "I-Thou," subject to subject modes as the texture of interaction. There is no "force field" impregnating, no "unilateral superpower," but a "relational force" that "lures" the other and others into fulfillment.[11] In another setting, the argument was advanced to talk of God as gentle. And strength and gentle need not be construed as at odds. In a sense, only the gentle are really strong. "The image of a gentle God of life affirms that everything is subject and nothing is object to God."[12]   And God is the eternal subject. God's agency aims at the well-being of others and the creation of just institutions in society.

When the footprint of empire defines agency, it obstructs God-talk which is relational and gentle.

Power, ambiguity, and agency are like a trinity in that they are distinguishable but interpenetrate each other.

We have been contending that empire creates a linguistic setting which serves to block God-talk. It clogs, distorts, the very categories in which God-talk transpires. And while we have suggested it blocks transcendent discourse, the argument can be made that empire distorts it whenever an attempt is made to engage in God-talk on terms set by empire. Then the power of God becomes a transcendent superpower who overwhelms. The ambiguity which preserves the transcendence of the transcendent gets translated as discernable in unmistakable terms ("God wanted me to bomb Iraq"). And the nature of agency in empire becomes one of denunciation and diminishes the self and its other relationships.

The church has not been mentioned since this introduction. Perhaps it is self-evident that it has a defining stake in whatever impedes God-talk and potentially distorts it. The church is where God-talk becomes real and is measured for authenticity. When God talk is at the margins, the church is forfeiting its identity.

Empire and Trails of Transcendence

There are at least several significant examples of God-talk in our contemporary setting which in very different ways aspire to trace the role of God in our national life. They are really polar opposites and form the parameters within which we will explore the relation of God to our history as a nation. Both, we will argue, are particularly susceptible to distortion by empire, indeed co-option by it. That is not to contend they are transparently false or ill-conceived. But they are subject to serving the interests of empire in destructive ways. At times the church invested its message in one or the other. One could think of them as symbolic authorization and unambiguous providence. The representatives of these positions for our purposes will be Robert Bellah and Stephen Webb.

In a 1967 article Robert Bellah reclaimed the notion of civil religion formerly identified with Rousseau (*The Social Contract*, Chapter 8, book 4).The Bellah article appeared in *Daedalus*, Winter 1967. In the piece Bellah argues "that there actually exists along side of and rather clearly differentiated from the churches an elaborate and well-institutionalized civil religion in America."[13] Bellah goes on to explain that "from the earliest years of the republic (there) is a collection of beliefs, symbols, and rituals with respect to sacred things and institutionalized in a collectivity. This religion ... was neither sectarian nor in any specific sense Christian."[14]

American civil religion begins in our "roots" and the value invested in our national existence and sanctioned by religious imagery. For Robert Bellah the text is the past and the task to resurrect the vision which has animated the nation. We are a people called from exile by God to communality. It is the force of our past which will renew us. Our possibilities are in a secure relationship to our promises as a nation with a religiously framed self-identity.

The responsibility of the scholar is to aid the process of synchronizing us with our past by drawing it into view. We are lost because there has been an eclipse of the religious meaning of our national life. In order to learn from our past and be transformed by it, the agenda is "... 1) that we search the whole tradition from its earliest beginnings... 2) that we subject everything we find to the most searching criticism, something that goes far beyond simply distinguishing the good tradition from the bad tradition... 3) that we open up our search entirely beyond the orbit of our own tradition..."[15] Our praxis is initially intellectual, a reflection which discerns our best heritage. American civil religion is a theology from above in that it proceeds from a formulation of the ideal to the circumstances at hand in anticipation of a different future.

Central to American civil religion is the premise that religion functions to integrate and enervate the nation. It appeals to spiritual resources for the formation of a communal consciousness and a sense of destiny. Clearly "... there is in American society a vague but real cluster of symbols, values, hopes and intimations of the transcendent which overarch our common life."[16] Their combined effect is to nurture a sense of "peoplehood" without which no nation can survive. Religion thus provides a political service through naming and symbolizing a spiritual foundation.

Given the religion/society model within American civil religion, it is important to explore the phenomenon of Christendom. We are apt to understand that term in relation to Constantine and eras in which the church became a controlling political force. But the phenomenon has more subtle forms, namely, when Christianity independent of the church is perceived as being that which orients the nation. The church is not empowered but its legitimating process is under the jurisdiction of the state. Then the Christian symbols do not function as a restraint but as a blessing. Once the symbols are out on loan to the nation, their function undergoes expansion. And there emerges the concept of a Christian nation along with Christian politicians and even Christian economics!

Certainly American civil religion is not seen by most of its advocates as ending in Christendom. Bellah and others want to maintain its capacity to mediate the prophetic element. The provision of a "sacred canopy" is not intended to immunize against criticism or to render inviolate the national practice. Rather, it is intended to enable and release the power of our best. But what follows is a slippery slope. Symbols once on loan for integrating soon are turned to sanctioning and then sacralizing.

American civil religion works from the premise of religion's functionality in society. Its task is to make the society work. One serious attempt to explore and defend American civil religion is a paper by John Coleman. Father Coleman begins with the contention that civil religion is "a functional universal: every nation has one."[17] Both individuals and corporate entities struggle with the issues of identity, vocation, and destiny. That places them in the orbit of religion where one grasps for its symbols and rituals. Furthermore, he argues, "...national experiences of threat, contingency, breakdown, and possible decline and death bring collectivities to a ... religious threshold."[18] The resources of faith become the tools for national self-affirmation and healing.

American civil religion unfortunately functions as what Paul Ricoeur calls an "ideological screen." It filters out. Because American civil religion begins in our identity as conveyed through our heritage, there is a measure of resistance to those realities which do not fit. Given the way we see ourselves, the tendency is to miss the data which work against our national self-perception. We cannot imagine our government might have complicity in the fall of Chile's Allende or that our purposes in Vietnam could be other than those formed by a commitment to freedom. The "cruel innocence" about which Michael Harrington writes may well be occasioned by our civil religion. Our ideology intercepts the cries of pain and the acts of perversion. It may also be that our civil religion fosters what Harrington calls "the *status quo* as utopia." Our sense of ourselves and what ought to be "is a visionary rationalization of present misery."[19] In a real sense the story told by American civil religion is the story we want told, free of contamination by the actuality of our circumstances.

The terse and contentious interaction between Jűrgen Moltmann and Robert Bellah is illustrative of the quality of the issues forged by American civil religion. Moltmann, conditioned by the German experience and the co-option of the religious community for political purposes, reads civil religion as having a mediating effect which only serves the interests of the state. He dismisses Bellah's proposal as "a relative justification of the *status quo*..."[20] Robert Bellah bristles under the charge of "a misplaced sacredness."[21] He alleges that the Nazi Germany syndrome is a blinder which intercepts responsible vision of his project. Bellah dismisses the critiques of Moltmann as "hostile polemic"[22] and protests that his critics invoke the worst examples of civil religion.

While the existence of American civil religion may be difficult to refute, its reality takes on significance in the face of empire. Even secularists in empire need to be wary of it. When ultimacy in any form is implicated, the issue of symbol lending is particularly perilous. At one extreme is the issue of "misplaced sacredness;" but any authorization of a nation's self-conception and action by religious imagery is problematic. American civil religion is a particularly choice prospect for cooption. The power of empire can readily invoke its "symbolic authorization" for imperial purposes. The church, as well, needs to retrieve the symbols for purposes congruent with the biblical tradition. The symbols need to be wedded to their origins and not available or subject to adoption for alien purposes.

While for Robert Bellah the content of transcendence tends to be more vague, some say empty, the content for Stephen Webb is explicit and evident.[23] As a sociologist, Bellah traces the ways in which religion appears in society; as a theologian, Webb explores the providential action of God. Webb knows who God is and what God is doing and where God is doing it. In particular he does not shy away from the rhetoric of providence and ascribing clear embodiments of it in our national life. It is anything but symbolic. In every sense, God is historized and God-talk has explicit references. Webb has no difficulty with particularity in God-talk.

Stephen Webb is fully invested in the "rhetoric of providence." In a sense, it is at the center of his theology and certainly his construction of God's relation to America. What cannot be disputed is the claim that God works in history towards ends God has promised. Those who dismiss the doctrine of providence in a real sense read God out of history. And they certainly leave the faith community without any connection to transcendence apart from the personal realm. Some conservatives are content with that and some more radical "lefties" applaud it. But it leaves the church without a rudder as it navigates in the public sphere. A God without a providential role in history becomes a spiritual mentor in the sky. And it leaves the Jesus we talk about later to function as a satellite without a home base. The biblical record clearly counts God a "player" in the events recorded in Scripture. Webb is on the mark when he claims, "The biblical narrative ... is a trustworthy account of what God has done, is doing, and will continue to do in the future. ...God's actions reveal God's nature."[24] One consequence of this is that Christians and the faith community are drawn into engagement. Being off stage in some mystical and spiritual trance is not an option. And Webb is right when he insists being apolitical is not an option for Christians.

Confidence in God's providential activity has been deflated by certain events in the experience of some and the memory of others.

Webb freely grants that theodicy (God's relation to evil) has taken a toll on providence.[25] The Holocaust and the experience of Blacks in America are cases in point. The long experience of the Jewish community, culminating in the death camps, would seem to render election a curse. And the claims of many theologians that the oppressed have a privileged place or setting would seem again to be an instance of abandonment. For whatever reasons, God did not or was not able to make good on God's promises. The implication is that God is not up to the tasks of moving history toward fulfillment. Webb is not distracted or detoured by those arguments. Rather, he finds imbedded in them the notion "of a tyrannical God who tries to smash our wills and restrict our freedom"[26] while not wanting to inflate human freedom or diminish God's influence in history. Webb sustains his confidence in providence with a "dialectic between blessing and judgment (which) needs to be carefully held together for providence to make good theological sense."[27] Hence God's providence and human freedom are not irreconcilable.

The problems in Webb's dedication to a legitimate doctrine begin to surface when he explores what God might be doing in America today. It is one thing to affirm that "Christians cannot be apolitical."[28] And it is reasonable to assert "God works through nations to achieve the divine plan …" [29] His position begins to be problematic when Webb claims "that America is doing more than any nation to spread the kinds of political structures that can best prepare the globe for God's ultimate work …"[30] There is, for Webb, an alignment between the purposes of God and the existence and action of America. Then the validity of providence has been collapsed into the American reality; providence now is who we are and what we do. Apparently God makes wise choices and we benefit. Then there is an alliance between patriotism and providence which Webb claims to avoid.[31]
It is interesting to note that when he considers "manifest destiny" he wants to distinguish it from providence. The distinction hinges on the reference from which nations acquires its mission. While admitting that providence is not singularly for the benefit of America

he asserts, "Where Manifest Destiny went wrong was in associating America with a New Rome rather than a New Israel."[32] Apparently it got the right point but the wrong reference.

The means by which God adopts America for providential purposes begins with the claim, "God places agents, both individual and collections, into position where they can do what God wants."[33] And the action or intervention is systematic as well. It may be shocking but not entirely off course to say that "Democracy is the fruit that falls closest to the Christian tree…"[34] and is a set up for a unifying posture in the global scene which could serve the purposes of church growth. However, invoking an economic factor as part of the providential plan is more than problematic. Webb wants to be clear that American Christianity and American-led capitalism are not on a par in terms of the ends or goals of history.[35] While making clear that the Kingdom of God and not America is the goal of history, Webb is bold to speculate that "The Kingdom of God might be ushered in by bankers and business people…"[36] Apparently consumption, free trade, and open markets are the gateway to the goal of history.

Up to this point we have not stroked the vulnerability of Webb's claim that America is the unique instrument and embodiment of God's providential work. But simply put, how better to use religion to legitimate global imperialism? Providence as described by Webb can become, or has become, an active agent of empire's aspiration. Empire is enhanced by the globalization of God.

While one could argue that Bellah's civil religion is susceptible to the purposes of empire, Webb's providential designation of America actually accomplishes it for empire. No seduction is necessary!

Transcendence and Contention
There is nothing new about the agenda of balancing the transcendence and immanence of God. The church through its theologians, in its worship, and as it faces the world struggles with that – or should, relentlessly. The issues tend to focus on a God who is out of this

world and one who is lost in it. What we have seen in the last section is God-talk which tends to legitimize and endorse the prevailing order. Walter Brueggermann referred to this as "the religion of the captive God in which all over-againstness is dissipated."[37] Perhaps another way to think about the issue is to ask, "How can the church historize God without horizontalizing God?"

It would not be unique or unusual to center God-talk on the Christ event. However, to focus on the interaction of Jesus and Thomas might be. The encounter is often dismissed as an instance of inappropriate doubt. Thomas had not been with the other disciples when Jesus appeared to them. And he was not prepared to take their word on the Risen Christ. "We have seen the Lord" (John 20:25) was not a sufficient witness. Eight days after the first appearance "Jesus came and stood among them" (vs. 26). Jesus addressed Thomas, "Put your finger here, and see my hands; and put your hand, and place it in my side; do not be faithless but believing" (vs. 27). While Jesus challenged Thomas there is a sense in which that disciple eventually got it right. The Risen Christ is still the Crucified Christ; the Risen Lord retains his wounds. The resurrection does not cancel the crucifixion. It is worth noting that it was Jesus who invited Thomas to touch the wounds! When Thomas responded "my Lord and my God" (vs. 28) there is a sense that immanence and transcendence are unified without contradiction. Only a wounded Lord is an image with which the church can stand against empire.

Authentic God-talk begins in the wounds. While the church says, "My Lord and my God," the wounds never heal. And authentic discourse is framed in that setting. "Our task is to find words… about God in the midst of the starvation of millions, the humiliation of races regarded as inferior, discrimination against women, … a persistent high rate of infant mortality, those who simply 'disappear' …"[38] Resistance to empire is generated by the understanding of a triumphant God imbedded in the wounds of the world. That God can never be captured by those who inflict the wounds. Jesus may have sounded harsh in responding to Thomas, but when Thomas claimed the Risen Christ the transcendence shed blood. Those who touch the point of crucifixion cannot worship or serve a God whose reality has been dissipated.

Those who live in the privileges and benefits of empire will dismiss Thomas as a doubter and proceed to "de-historize Jesus." A heavenly Christ can do no earthly harm to the regime. But a Christ with wounds draws all the wounded of the world into the divine reign and stands in resistance. The crucified Christ – some say the "executed Christ" – cannot be separated from the reality of existence in history of those who are victims of empire. When the church says, "My Lord and My God" to the wounded/Risen One it is committed to what John Dominic Crossan calls "The Great Divine Cleanup of this world."[39] The encounter of Jesus and Thomas puts the empire on notice about the imbeddedness of that transcendent God. That God moves through the events of history – without being identified with any of them – with purposes which exalt the lowly and bring down the powerful. The empire cannot capture that God because that God is purging its D.N.A. of control.

But the wounded can see what the wounders cannot. Those who "live in the wounds of history ..."[40] can claim the Risen Christ without "de-historizing him" and embrace him as the agent of their resistance to empire. They can name God because of their partnership with God, not God's partnership with them as in Webb. Jesus' cross is their cross and the empty tomb is the ground of their hope. There transcendence is made present and the masks of empire are exposed. The victims see themselves in the wounds of the cross and they at the same time map the future made possible by the Risen One. And they are "Like an inverted mirror in which the First World, on seeing itself disfigured, comes to know itself in truth."[41] Cooption of the Divine presence is not an option. Neither is exaltation into some heavenly realm. Thus our "walk in history," the churches' walk in history, is one of daily resistance to the multiple forms in which empire would define reality and create systems and institutions to enforce it.

In *The Sorrows of Empire*, Chalmers Johnson documents "a dangerous change in the thinking of some of our leaders, who began to see our republic as a genuine empire… no longer bound by international law, the concerns of allies, or any contrasts on its use of military force."[42] And he concludes, "Since 9/11, our country has undergone a transformation … which may well be irreversible."[43] That, alas, is a secular projection! It does not recognize the penetration of the Transcendent One. God-talk is secure when the Risen Christ invited Thomas to touch the wounds.

SCRIPTURE, THE CHURCH, AND EMPIRE

CHAPTER THREE

Introduction

Scripture can be read without reference to empire. Typically, in the church it is. Preachers, laypersons, and even scholars focus on the written text searching for "the message," perhaps some inspiration, or at least ethical guidance. Empire does not protrude in the process of interpretation. Neither does some other framework, or so it seems. Words mean what they mean, right? In the summer of 2009 a southern Governor was forced to admit a marital indiscretion. Reference was made in the press to "C Street, a Washington dormitory for lawmakers funded by a highly secretive Christian organization called 'the Fellowship.'" The Governor acknowledged membership and his involvement in Bible study there. A resident revealed the nature of the study group saying, "Somebody'll share a verse..."[1] The implication is that a text of Scripture floats like a verbal artifact and lands on ears poised to receive it without compromise or complexity. This unexamined assumption is that there is no necessary correlation between content and context. Words, in a sense, are naked; they are void of history, tradition, or culture. Words communicate in a straight forward manner. They mean whatever they say.

In contemporary terms, many would understand that who said the words, his or her life experiences, contribute to legitimate understanding of their meaning. For example, President Obama is often referred to as a powerful orator, even by those who disagree with him. Some in the Academy might say he is a "wordsmith." One commentator on CNN argued that the President is really a "great explainer" rather than "great orator." Consider Obama's explanations of complex issues in the years 2008-2009. When he talked about race, he invoked the memory of his white Grandparents who were instrumental in his upbringing. When he talked about religion he explored what drew him to the Trinity Church when he was a young lawyer and organizer. When he talked about education the priorities of his Father and the persistence of his Mother were in it. When he talked about his political agenda and style, he drew forward his early years as an advocate for the disadvantaged on the South side of Chicago. One can listen to his words but really understanding them requires attention to his life experiences that generated them. Often those who want to diminish his intentions sever the connection between the words and the setting that gave rise to them.

Text and Context

It is no different with an authentic reading of Scripture. Bible study, preaching, or daily reading ought not to be about "sharing a verse" and letting it communicate without reference to the setting which shaped it. Richard H. Horsley says it bluntly: "Text cannot be considered apart from context."[2] Who said it, to whom, under what circumstances all factor in to understanding the words? It is curious that Christians, who cannot imagine a church without a building, worship without a minister, or faith without creeds, think of Scripture without a context. The presumption is that the Bible in fact speaks for itself and that a willing listener really hears the intended message. Church, tradition, faith are all embodied; they are not abstractions. Scripture is embodied as well. The content is immersed in a context which shapes its meaning. "Contrary to popular opinion, the bible does not speak for itself. Rather, interpretations of biblical texts and reconstructions of early Christian history are shaped by the contemporary interests... of the biblical historian (or the) general reader just as much as they were by people in the first century."[3] It is difficult to imagine communities of faith who would recognize that "the bible does not speak for itself." Sermons, Bible studies, and dialogues on faith usually proceed by "somebody'll share a verse" and they are on to its meaning. When one thinks of some of the horrendous things that have been done by Christians and the church, often as not a verse is shared and an evil is authorized. As we have explored elsewhere, slavery and the Holocaust are classic examples. To get the words "right," context and text need to be negotiated. Context sheds light on content and sets boundaries within which meaning emerges.

The church has been complicit in lending or attaching Scripture to inappropriate events or circumstances and most frequently, our national life. In other chapters we have dealt with the claim that America is "the new Israel," that we are in fact "the promised land," that we serve the world as a "beacon on a Hill," that we have achieved the status of a "chosen people." And it all supports the notion that we have a privileged place in the Divine economy. Whether or not those labels are appropriate hinges on an examination of context. And that requires a rigorous attention both to the context of biblical times as well as our own. But the issue lingers about whether or not empire is the context which surfaces the content.

Richard A. Horsley makes the bold claim that "Christianity was a product of empire... (It) started as an anti-imperial movement... Jesus catalyzed a movement of the renewal of Israel."[4] The reference to "renewal of Israel" surfaces the realization he did not emerge in a vacuum. Those who heard his words and witnessed his actions had a "social memory." The center piece of that shared memory was the exodus events and the covenant that emerged from them. The Israelites were liberated from the Egyptians and Pharaoh. They were brought, lead out of bondage, to a promised land. There was what Horsley calls "a rich Israelite cultural tradition"[5] which resonated with the message and ministry of Jesus. And resistance to empire was embedded in the community members who heard his speech. "The beatitudes and woes, the covenantal blessing and curses, like the 'symbolic reversals of faith religion,' constitute the equivalent of a radical counter-ideology."[6] And it focuses on the ideology of domination formerly and in the twenty-first century. Horsley also notes, as we develop elsewhere, "The very action of celebrating the Lord's Supper in commemoration of the renewal of the Mosaic covenant would have constituted an act of resistance by a community of resistance."[7] The "social memory" of domination and resistance was rehearsed in the sacrament. The deliverance by a liberating God is the context and co-ordinate of the content in the emergence of Christianity from the Jesus event. Those who heard and witnessed had ears and a lens shaped by the discernment of oppressors and the emergence of liberation. To read the words and deeds as in the rise of Christianity without reference to empire is to treat them as religious artifacts which can drift into endorsing the prevailing order and its structure of institution of domination.

Jesus and Empire

It will strengthen our argument about empire as a co-ordinate of content if we attend to the ways in which empire is the consistent fact in the Jesus event. But there is a text and an event which stand in the way of that; and it merits our attention.

Those who want to sustain a privatized view of Jesus – as one simply connected to one's spiritual and ethical life – and aspire to draw a clear line between religion and politics, appeal confidently to Mark's Gospel. There, they claim, is the Kingdom of God on the one hand and the rule of Caesar on the other. And they are separated and non-contesting realities. The Pharisees and Herodias, of which they were often agents, set up the test for Jesus in regard to paying the obligatory tribute to Caesar and the empire (Mark 12:13-17). "Is it lawful to pay taxes (tribute) to Caesar or not? Should we pay them or not?" Jesus asked for a coin: "Whose likeness and inscription is on this?" When they answered "Caesar's" Jesus responded, "Render to Caesar the things that are Caesar's, and to God the things that are God's." The expectation had been that Jesus would explicitly negate tributes to Caesar. He did not. But those who heard his words with a "social memory" heard a different message. And it was one that claimed everything – social, economic, political – for God. "His reply was a bold, as well as clever, declaration of independence from Roman imperial rule."[8] Everything belongs to God and nothing to Caesar. God alone is God! The followers of Jesus knew exactly what he meant. And so should we and the church in 2011. The empire has no legitimate claim. No loyalty and no possessions were owed to Caesar. The alleged separation of religion and politics is nullified. God has only one Son and loyalty is singularly to him.

That said, we can proceed and note that empire exerts a persistent claim on Jesus. And it begins at the beginning in the birth narrative. The event is simply not the charming, endearing, and inspiring one portrayed in the Christmas season. The footprint of empire is on it. "A decree went out from Caesar Augustus that all the world should be enrolled" (Luke 2:1). This may sound like an innocent census, but it was not. The census was for the purpose of establishing the taxes and tribute which oppressed the people. The Roman Empire was exacting disproportionate claims upon the meager produce of the people. And this baby was destined to be a "savior" – the role rightfully claimed by the emperor. And what did Herod do when he heard about the threat to the regime of which he was a client? He sent his terrorists out to destroy all the male babies under two years of age (Matthew 2:1-18). It does not take much imagination to see the threat to the regime in the words upon the lips of Mary: "he has put down the mighty from their thrones, and exalted those of low degree; …" (Luke 1:52). Little blonde hair, blue-eyed Mary was passionate in her expectation of what God was initiating. Resistance to empire began in a manger. "Jesus is born into a world of violent, all-encompassing imperial control, where Emperor Augustus is registering the whole world for purposes of taxation. Those taxes would then fund his military in service of Roman "peace" maintained by an army quick enough to stamp out any dissention or discord."[9] The task of the faith community is to be in that world but not endorse it.

Or consider the Temple. Is it not the "church" where Jesus rather prematurely said he was about his Father's business and when ready for the ministry read the Bible? How many times has one in the church today heard the Temple referenced to as "a visible reminder of Roman domination, the primary face of Roman imperial rule?"[10] Or that the reverends were appointed by Roman rulers? Or that it was where taxes were collected, perhaps more accurately extorted? And wasn't the Temple cleansing episode like a rather intemperate attack on Friday night bingo at the local Catholic Church? The reality is that the Temple was more like the bank, city hall, mayor's court, and the street division all rolled into one with some men in clerical collars in evidence! It was the center of exploitation. And remember that John the Baptist was arrested and beheaded when he demanded covenantal justice, justice grounded in Israel's relation to God, (Mark 6:17-29) which the temple preempted. In a very real sense, empire centered in the Temple. Jesus not only condemned the Temple but announced its inevitable destruction. It was "the ultimate act of blasphemy and profanation of the sacred central institution of the political-economy of Judea… the instrument of Roman rule…"[11] The cleansing of the Temple – far from being a reaction to bingo – was a frontal attack on empire. And when one folds in the persistent connection between the crucifixion of Jesus and his attacks on the Temple, it becomes clear that empire was the dominant cause of his death. The fact that the golden eagle, the symbol of imperial rule, hung over the gate of the Temple ought to silence any claim for the separation of church and state! Jesus in relation to the Temple seals the role of empire in his life and death.

It would be difficult to deny that the things of the Kingdom of God, or the Reign of God, were central to the teaching of Jesus. And it goes a long way toward understanding why he was a threat to the dominant order. To affirm the Reign of God is to gut the claim of empire. And there is no way in which the Kingdom of God rhetoric can be rendered safe discourse. Especially in his parables, Jesus set the Reign of God over against the reign of Caesar. That the world is ruled by God and not Caesar, that the one who announced the coming of the Kingdom was alleged to be the Son of God and not Caesar, and that the disposition of history was in the jurisdiction of the God of Israel was a direct threat – and one that had to be answered, eventually with the cross. The parables of Jesus were social commentary; they constituted a narrative critique of the empire. In every sense they were subversive. "Jesus used parables to present situations familiar to the rural poor, to encode the system of oppression that controlled their lives and held them in bondage."[12] They spoke to everyday life in ways the imperial order found de-stabilizing at the very least. The control of the established order was rigorously contested. Consider the parable of the vineyard laborers. They are expendable. The pay of a denarius was anything but generous; the owners were in a position to suppress payments for labor; and the capacity to discriminate without justification was limitless. The end result of the inequitable distribution was to turn the laborers against each other and preclude any organizing to secure rights. The coming Reign of God is not like that and will destroy it. The incongruity is etched in unmistakable terms. Every system of oppression will be ended with the coming Kingdom about which Jesus preached in parables. Jesus exposed the empire and proclaimed that God would bring an end to it as an agent of exploitation.

Considering the cross and the events leading up to it seals the contention with empire. Here the footprint of empire is more like a stampede! It is crucial to understand that the crucifixion is not like the electric chair in our time. At one level it is more like the lynching of Blacks during slavery. Tom Thatcher reminds us "that Roman crucifixion was driven more by the theorem 'every punishment has less to do with the offense than with the example.'"[13] In order to have that effect it is apt to occur in the most populated or heavily traveled areas so that the intended fears had the most opportunity to be instilled. The empire wants to establish its ultimate jurisdiction over life and death. What better way to establish power? But Thatcher's comment does not just get at the full meaning of crucifixion in Jesus' time. It was invoked for persons believed to be subversive in relation to the empire. Stoning was the execution of choice in the instances of blasphemy. Crucifixion is the premier act of the state in establishing its control. Horsley argues that "the crucifixion of Jesus is, after all, one of the most unequivocally political events recorded in the New Testament."[14] Jesus is crucified as one dangerous to the interests of the empire. That does not detract from the impact on others. It is an act of terror. But Jesus is not innocent!

It is interesting to remember that it was Judas who brought the soldiers to seize Jesus. He did not invoke the religious establishment to bring charges of heresy. But it is more important to focus on Pilate. That establishes the political nature of the trial and subverts the heinous attempt to "blame the Jews" which achieved prominence in the Holocaust. Attention to John 18:23-19:22 draws into unambiguous focus the interaction between one who represents the interests of the empire and the one whose message subverted its claim in announcing the coming Reign of God. While some have depoliticized the event and the role of Pilate, that does not correspond to the reality of the interaction. "The Jesus-Pilate scene continues ... the task of imperial negotiation. It presents direct oppositional interaction between Jesus and the empire as Jesus and Pilate meet face to face before an alliance of empire's ruling elite crucifies Jesus."[15] Then, as we have argued elsewhere, Easter morning robs death of its power and exposes the empire as finally powerless before the purposes of God. That is about as political as it gets. Ultimately, empire is shredded.

Jesus would not be who he was if understood apart from empire. Ironically, it is that excision that enables empire to co-opt him for its purposes, or at least drive him to the sidelines as a silent partner.

Empire and the Early Church
And the early church would not be what it was if excised from its interaction with empire. While it has been argued that Christianity cannot be understood apart from its interface with empire, neither

can the Jesus movement and its more institutionalized community. One obvious place to begin is with a sense of what the New Testament means by church. It definitely is not a sequestered spiritual sanctuary where persons divest themselves of worldly considerations. Some would accept that without embracing any worldly role for the church. Nurturing salvation is the appropriate realm and agenda. But that does not fit with the Greek word translated church: *ekklesia*. It "literally means the democratic assembly and is best translated 'democratic congress' of full decision making citizens."[16] The root meaning of *ekklesia* is democracy, a space where decision-making is shared and equality is paramount. Justice and egalitarian relations prevail. It is a place where all "are equal but not the same."[17] Reciprocity persists and solidarity is evident. One cannot avoid the conclusion that *ekklesia* is political, in a radically democratic sense. That puts the church on a collision course with empire. It serves the interests of the privileged and powerful. And it exploits without regret and dominates without guilt. The interests of the many are subordinated to those of the ruling class in empire.

Part of what made the church so threatening as it emerged in response to the Jesus event was the degree to which a renewal of the covenant was a persistent focus. "If anything, he (Jesus) intensified the covenant demands for communal cooperation and mutual aid, to love enemies, be good, and lend liberally."[18] And the covenant was with a liberating God for whom justice and peace were a consistent agenda. To be reminded of who God is, is to be reminded of who the community is called to be. "The Mosaic covenant thus provided the fundamental framework and principles for community life in the villages of Israel."[19] And that required entirely new political, social, economic relations than those imposed by the ruling order. Empire was clearly at odds with the terms of daily life in which justice, dignity, and solidarity were the agenda. A space of generosity and sharing was a form of interaction the empire could not tolerate. A political entity with transformed social interaction puts the *ekklesia* on a collision course with empire. People taking control of their lives and being responsible for the *shalom* of others was the antithesis of empire and could not be tolerated by it. It was insurrectionary, anti-imperial, and grounded in the resurrection that spelled the doom of empire. The church is the community with a counter-ideology to the one in empire. And one can't understand the church of New Testament times apart from its resistance and discernment of empire. Whenever community lives the resurrection everything else is vulnerable and susceptible to the purposes of God.

The early church was not a carping community, fully invested in bemoaning the prevailing conditions. It boldly and intentionally positioned itself at the intersection of realities where people were marginalized and oppressed and announced the purposes of God. A disconnection with institutions created by empire was not an option. It not only embraced the victims but countered the instruments of victimization. The proclamation of the Reign of God meant that poverty was a religious issue, taxation and tribute enforced by Temple functions were religious issues, and terrorist activities engendering fear were religious issues. The Jesus movement and the early church put the Body of Christ on the line. "In teaching people to pray for the Kingdom of God, he focused on the most basic and urgent economic matters: enough food to eat, day by day, and the cancelation of the debts that were threatening the basis of their livelihood."[20] As we will consider in the chapter on worship, the crucified Christ merged with the crucified people. The individualism characteristic of the western world and church was totally alien to those who were gathered in response to Jesus. The continuation of the incarnation meant total immersion in the world's pain and resistance to those who inflicted it. Exodus church did not mean leaving the world but leaving subservience to the empire and its agencies. While the early church and Jesus movement was not the Kingdom of God, they were agents of intrusion in the world empire created and sustained. It was in every sense a counter-community with a counter-ideology committed to establishing a counter-world, egalitarian and mutually supportive. Truly, it was a direct challenge to empire and its determination to create reality in a world that served its interests alone. In the Epilogue we will re-examine the role of the church as a counter-community in our time.

In summary, Scripture locates the church – then and now – in the midst of empire with a vocation to serve the purposes of God, confident that the Reign of God is just and victorious. What could be more destabilizing to empire?

RHETORIC
AND RESISTANCE

CHAPTER FOUR

Introduction

In the chapter on transcendence, we explored how empire affects the categories relevant for God-talk. It occupies them in ways that block essential meanings for the manner in which God can be understood as present in history. Here the agenda is broader and perhaps more elusive. The assertion that empire defines reality – or aspires to – includes the sense it defines the language emerging from it. There is a linguistic entrapment, encapsulation, which assures words mean what empire says they do. While Shriver does not explicitly talk about empire, his agenda to redefine patriotism is a case in point. For those viewing through the lens of empire, patriotism and uncompromising loyalty are synonymous. You consent rigorously to the agenda of the country or you are unpatriotic, disloyal. By contrast, Shriver's patriotism includes and values dissent. Love of country is evident in the willingness to surface flaws and failures. In the discourse of the religious right, (which often overlaps with empire and becomes an agent of it) providence and patriotism are correlated.

Another way to state the issue is to note that the empire has one set of transcripts and the church another. They tell contesting stories about reality. James C. Scott, in a different context, explores "public transcripts" and "hidden transcripts." The public ones are of those controlling the dominant order while the hidden ones embrace various forms of resistance.[1] Clearly, empire is the "public transcript." There might be some reluctance to think of the faith community's transcripts as hidden, but biblical scholar Walter Brueggemann thinks of it as a "minority report," indeed a subversive one. The church is the community which aspires to live God's reality and to embrace the language that flows from it. In the first instance, it is created by that reality (the Coming Kingdom/Reign of God) and language emerges from it. Unfortunately, as we have seen in civil religion, the faith community's language can be borrowed and used for alien purposes. Then, empire penetrates and perverts the discourse. Seeing America as "the New Israel" or as a "city on the hill" is classic image theft. The narrative construal of empire violates the metaphor/image and puts it in the service of empire's agenda.

It is interesting to note that there are instances when the faith community poaches on the language of empire and establishes linguistic contestation. Richard A. Horsley documents this[2] in the writings of the apostle Paul. There is a conspicuous illustration of anti-imperial rhetoric or what Scott calls the "work of negation"[3] which challenges the rhetoric of "ideological domination" with the freedom of the hidden transcript.[4] More specifically, Horsley surfaces how the early Christians in the letters ascribed to Paul actually co-opt and usurp the language of the empire. The gospel referenced in the Roman imperial world was Caesar's message of peace and security and the emperor was the savior. He brought salvation.[5] Faith (*pistis*) centered on the empires' Lord. Paul talked about the Jesus event in terminology reserved for Caesar. The assemblies (*ekkesia*) represented those cities where Caesar ruled supreme but it became for Paul the metaphor for the church community. Horsley goes on to say that "By applying this key imperial language to Jesus Christ, Paul was making him into the alternative or real emperor of the world, the head of an anti-imperial institutional alternative society."[6] Thus, the church with this rhetoric was "acting contrary to the decrees of Caesar" (Acts 17:7). It was an act of subversion, head on contestation.

The Poor as Linguistic-Setting

While the church in our time has often been identified with the middle class and exploited by the dominant order, the message of the early church is summarily situated in the plight of the poor. Third World theologians name the faith community as "the church of the poor" (which it is) but for our purposes that does not represent the typical American church. At best, it may be a mix of classes; that is both its blessing and its bane. But, in contrast with the empire, the authentic church exists in an environment saturated by the interests of the poor. The message is inseparable from them and cannot be fathomed apart from them. It is in the encounter with the poor and the response to them that the message of faith is constructed and communicated. Their needs and aspirations prevail in the Christian message. They are at the center of Christianity. Everything pivots on and through them.

When Jesus inaugurated his ministry in the Temple, drawing upon the words of Isaiah (61:1-2), he claimed he was anointed "to preach good news to the poor" (Luke 4:18). In the eyes of some, that might be a way of acknowledging they needed it. The reality is that they alone would receive it! Jon Sobrino quotes Jeremias: "The Kingdom of God belongs *only* to the poor."[7] Since this is "God's option" it is "unappealable."[8] God passes through this world in the lives of the poor, not because they are perfect or pure, but because they have "received 'new' ears for hearing the word which is from God … and 'new' eyes for seeing God …"[9] While some would claim the church has a ministry to the poor, the Gospel is that the poor *are* the ministry. They are the capsule in which the message is embedded. Indeed, salvation is inseparable from them. And the task of the church is to receive from them rather than give to them.[10] It is in entering their reality, in solidarity with their struggle, and in openness to the Word of which they are vessels that the church and Christians can approach the throne of grace. Jesus put it bluntly: "I was hungry and you gave me food, I was thirsty and you gave me drink, I was a stranger and you welcomed me, I was naked and you clothed me, I was in prison and you came to me" (Matthew 25:35). It is not that the poor hold "the keys to the Kingdom" but they are the Kingdom in the sense God and Jesus are present in them. No bypass is possible. There is no access to God apart from them and no salvation that is not with them. In other language, the Reign of God and the reality of the poor are correlates.

While the presence of God in the poor is at the center of the biblical faith, they are not an inert constituency. In the framework of empire the poor have a remarkable history. Along with all those empire has marginalized and dehumanized, they ultimately refuse to be subordinated. In a remarkable study of empire, Timothy Parsons documents that over time empires are "unsustainable because their subjects find them intolerable."[11] Successful resistance has a vivid trail and is undisputable. While Parsons as an historian does not connect the presence of God in the poor with the history of rebellion, theologians are likely to do so. This happens where God is lodged – at least to the eyes of faith. There is another factor that plays into this in the west and it is the emergence of the nation-state during the eighteenth century. Those who were subjected and dehumanized did more than protest the intolerable conditions. Their revolt ultimately gave rise to a political consciousness and form. The rise of nationalism eroded the claims of empire; in a sense, it voided them. Revolt has political consequence. At the least one could claim that the rebellion of the victims and the political transformation provided the impulses with which the God of freedom could navigate.

There is a sense in which the poor keep the church on message. And that is both a threat and a challenge to empire. As long as the transcript of the Christian message and community is grounded in the poor, it is immune to the advances and enticements of the transcript of the empire. Christendom is not an option. When one thinks, for example, of two more egregious realities – slavery and the Holocaust – one cannot escape the realization that lynching took place after church over picnics, and some clergy authorized Hitler

53

by their presence in his inner circle. That could only happen because the faith community casts off its anchor. When anchored in the poor, floating is not an option and endorsing cannot transpire.

That could not be more different from the posture and position of empire. It focuses on the elite, their privileges and their power. Those with positions in empire control reality for others, and the poor in particular. They are submerged in a culture that empire creates and dominates. And the obligation of the majority is to conform and be complicit in the agenda of empire. They are only free to choose what has been chosen for them. One might not normally or legitimately think of the middle class, for example, as oppressed. But they are powerless.[12] The public transcript sets the conditions in which we function. And our destiny does not flow from *our* visions and energies, but from loyalty to the purposes of empires' agenda. The transcript of empire subordinates and from its interests there is no refuge. This may be what Scott calls a "mask" behind which the empire seems beneficent and a mask behind which the people seem to benefit.[13] More to the point, Scott argues that "the dominant never control the stage absolutely, but their wishes normally prevail. In the short run, it is in the interest of the subordinate to produce a more or less credible performance, speaking the lines and making the gestures he knows are expected of him."[14] While that might seem to be too stark a statement, simply note the limited tolerance of the empire for reflection much less even modest doses of protest. It is "un-American."

In this context the significance of the church becomes clear. For one thing, the church anchored in the reality of the poor unmasks the empires' agenda. Because it knows who is really King, it knows who is not. The church can name the pretenders. But more significantly, it has institutional counter-power. Individuals standing up for the hidden transcript are significant and inspirational. But a community living a different transcript is both threatening and subversive. What is unique about the faith community is that it only needs to embrace the favor of God and be emboldened by the faith that God prevails. The resurrection follows the crucifixion and the wounded God triumphs in history. But it is a history rooted in the life of the poor.

Sin and Resistance

Over time the church has had an uneasy relationship with a doctrine of sin. Currently, the religious right has tended to overdose on it while the liberals have had an attraction to a more optimistic view of human nature. And some of those distinctions have become distractions because they associated sin either exclusively or predominantly with the personal sphere. It is a function of failures and flaws in the behavior of individuals. And Jesus is perceived as the one who washes our personal sins away. But, "sin has a historical dimension."[15] While it is personal, it needs to be understood as social as well. James Cone states in similar terms: sin is a "communal concept."[16] It includes the formations of the world which are organized against the purposes of God. In the final analysis, then, sin is a political concept which names where the nation blocks the purposes of God and yields to the goals of empire.

There is a sense in which sin is an alien concept for empire. As noted earlier, empire has no tolerance for ambiguity; its agenda is not subject to flaws. Its goals are not marred by compromises and its means toward them are not in conflict with them. The posture of empire and its rhetoric are marked by arrogance. Part of the effectiveness of empire is its confidence "it got it right." If one looks back to our section on the Iraq war and other statements by President Bush, the purity of our aspirations and the innocence of our strategies were evident in remarkable ways. President Bush has an intense personal sense of sin but no public one. And he capped his foreign policy with divine authorization: "God wanted me to bomb Iraq." Empire cannot put sin in circulation in history and its purposes for it. For empire, salvation and selfishness are congenial, even essential to the agenda of domination.

Jon Sobrino makes it clear that "sin is that which deals death."[17]

It is what dehumanizes. Certainly that can be interpersonal and subjective interaction. More pervasively it is structural and institutional. Sin is creating a world that produces victims and sustains a culture of victimization; it is a negation of God's passage in history among the powerless. Sin is "an economy with no thought for the *oikos*; an arms race with no thought of life; international trade… with no thought of fairness; the destruction of nature with no thought of Mother Earth; manipulated and false information with no thought for truth…"[18] Sin appears when empire emerges in structural and institutional dehumanization; it is consenting to their presence. And it is being at odds with what God is doing in history.

If "sin is that which deals death" then it is thwarting the God of life. Jesus said, "I come that they may have life, and have it abundantly" (John 10:6). And life is food to nourish, shelter from the elements, education for advancement, protection from abuse. God does not build empires; empires oppose God. The God of life creates spaces and resources that enable human development and fulfillment. The God of life enables truth to emerge from deception and manipulation. The God of life calls forth institutions which sustain rather than diminish. "There is no life without eating, drinking, healthy housing, liberty and affection or acceptance."[19] To oppose those projects is sin; salvation is solidarity with the victims of them.

The rhetoric of empire does not embrace issues of social justice but legitimates injustices as "the cost of doing business." Racism, sexism, heterosexism, homophobia are not on the empires' plate or field of interest. But they are for the faith community. Indeed, they are among the poor, the victims who suffer from the power and privileges of the elite. Their dehumanization is sin and defeating it is part of salvation – God's movement on earth through God's people. The task of the church is not to create a sin free world; that would be impossible. But to create a world where social sin has been unmasked and the space of freedom has been enlarged. The task of the church is humanization not simply because it is needed but because God is doing it. The risen Christ still has wounds and they are evident in the victims of empire. The church must not only name the demons but be the community whose rhetoric resists and subverts the empire that produces them.

When we think of sin as social, it may be one of the most important images in the "work of negation," the rhetoric of a reality that comes from God. Awareness of the social forms of sin is not only agenda-setting but calls the community to attention before them. Sin at the same time equips the faith community to resist cooption by empire and consort with its purposes. Knowing that salvation comes from God enables the community of faith to stand apart and stand against the world of domination and the ideologies that authorize it. Absent a healthy embrace of sin, the church can yield to false utopias and exploitive means of reaching them. The totalization promised by empire is unmasked and its agenda subverted by a community with a healthy sense of sin.

The Future as Preservation or Possibility

We have been contending that rhetoric which is lodged in the reality of the poor and acknowledges the phenomenon of sin is significant in the resistance to empire. Reclaiming that language is essential. As Sobrino argues "we must struggle to take back control of words and their definition, so that future direction for the human community will not be set by the language of empire (of power, triumph, superiority, contempt) but by the language of God (compassion, unguarded truth, brotherhood, utopia)."[20] And it is on the issue of the future we need to contend now.

Both empire and the church have a fixation on the future. It is an essential ingredient in the tradition of both. Utopia in some sense is at the heart of both transcripts. But what characterizes those futures and does it decisively differentiate them? The distinction is between the future as preserved for empire, and the future as possibility for the church. Reflecting on the world of Pompey and Augustus, Richard Horsley notes that peace and prosperity, indeed a civilized society, was sustained by Pax Romana. It, "enabled the Romans to extract goods from the people they had subjected, in the form of tribute, in order both to support their military forces and to pacify the Roman masses with 'bread and circus'."[21] If we think back to our consideration of The Project for the New American Century and its implementation in the second Bush administration, the echo of that is vibrant. In a sense, the only agenda is to perpetuate the prevailing order and to secure the forces to insure America remains number one. While "what is good for us" internally has some distinct legitimacy, the imposition of that on others is problematic – imperialistic, in fact. The document on defense is geared toward a future in which no other nation emerges to challenge the American super power. In a very real sense, there is no future under empire because it is geared toward preserving privilege, our privilege. The future is selfish and self-serving and created to ensure nothing new arises. Obviously a future without newness is no future but focused on an eternal now. For empire the future is empty of possibilities and is sorely to the advantage of the advantaged. The goal is to make the present permanent.

By contrast, the transcript of the church is about inordinate possibilities. It sees the present as loaded with the interests of privilege and calls forth resistance. One of the recurrent lines in the work of Ignatio Ellacuria is "take responsibility for reality" along with "bearing the burden of reality."[22] And reality in this sense is unreal; the configurations of the world are consistently involving entrapment for the poor and other victims. The argument of Ellacuria calls up the memory of The Theology of Hope which Jürgen Moltmann wrote after his Nazi experience. Arguing against acquiescence to the present disorder and what is perceived to be reality, "Those who hope in Christ can no long put up with reality as it is, but begin to suffer under it, to contradict it. Peace with God means conflict with the world, for the goad of the promised future stabs inexorably into the flesh of every unfulfilled present."[23] Moltmann is not calling for optimism but for confidence in an "arriving God." And the future looks like what we have seen in the Jesus event. The future is really future and there are in a sense "whiffs" of it in the present. Its power is its presence as future not appearance.

The transcript of the church is threatening and disruptive precisely because it focuses on the Reign of God which is always coming and never embodied in any given institution or society. The empire thinks it is. By contrast, the imperial order stands under judgment. The Reign of God summons this realization and thus the contradiction of reality. There is an escape from captivity which occurs when the word is out that God's future has canceled the present realties and a community is called to live that future. The irony is that the victims, the poor, are the center of gravity in the "new world order." It comes about precisely because in them the truth about reality becomes apparent and a foretaste of the future is present in their resistance. The Reign of God, the Kingdom of God, means the future is coming by the grace of God and the prevailing privilege will be upended. And it is hope in the face of a seemingly hopeless situation. "In the conviction that the kingdom of God was at hand, he (Jesus) pressed a program of social revolution to reestablish just egalitarian and mutually supportive social-economic relations in the village communities that constituted the basic form of the people's life."[24] The transcript of the church is, the future is at hand, but never fully embodied in the present. And that rhetoric cancels the preservation agenda of the empire. Nothing is more threatening than a future over which you have no control. And the victims of the empire are agents of its coming from God. Oppression and exclusiveness have no future; and no present power.

The church that reclaims the rhetoric of the future can never collapse its transcript into the terms of the dominant one.

The Rhetoric of Grace and Social Control

There is a significant point at which the poor, sin, and the future intersect, and draw upon the same phenomenon. It might seem to be an unlikely place. At the intersection grace, forgiveness, intrudes and penetrates. Grace means the past can be cast into the past, bondage can be unleashed, and hopelessness can be contradicted. With grace the poor can be released from the cycles of oppression, sin can be acknowledged and blunted, and the future can be opened to unimaginable possibilities.

For empire, nothing is more important than control. Its aspiration to manage history in its own interest is relentless and pervasive. Empire aspires to an "iron cage" where nothing escapes it, nothing opens a gate; light is excluded. We have noted that the crucifixion of Jesus was in the first century empire's finest hour, most conclusive event. Often, it has been privatized and when limited to a sacrifice for personal sins, it is innocuous. Not so when read in context. If rigorously centered in history and interpreted faithfully, the meaning is political. While crucifixion then was also a means of disposing of undesirables, it was "much more importantly, a carefully orchestrated public performance that reenacted the story of Roman conquest... this individual (Jesus) symbolized his entire society's submission and defeat."[25] It was a decisive way for empire to clarify that it was in control – and there is no way to escape its jurisdiction. Controlling death is the ultimate sign of power.

Hannah Arendt raises the question of what it is about Jesus which makes him so threatening – even if there is no divine factor. Clearly, it was not the size of his following. It was not the wisdom of his teaching or the winsomeness of his person. And it was not even the performance of miracles. It was the capacity to forgive, the liberating grace in his ministry, by word and by deed. By contrast, "The refusal to forgive (or the management of the machine of forgiveness) amounts to enormous social control."[26] Empire thrives on entrapment, encapsulation in its agenda. Empire aspires to create a society where persons live in the consequences of their behaviors against the dominant order, and are never free of them. The failure to acquiesce to the empire's agenda is unforgiveable and therefore permanent condemnation. Absent grace, the present will always be permanent and free of dispute. The victims will always be victimized and the oppressor will always prevail. When forgiveness intrudes, it is unambiguously political. Its presence is an inevitable challenge to the prevailing order. For with empire's agenda, there can be no grace.

Grace, by contrast, is the handmaiden of the future, the necessary condition of a new future. While the resurrection of Jesus is the ultimate "trump" of empire's rule, one of the words of Jesus on the cross is transformative and therefore threatening: "Father, forgive them ..." (Luke 23:24). In the very midst of the triumph of empire, the reality of grace sets in and diminishes the occasion. The victory of empire is canceled in the moment of its apparent triumph. Empire is served by the claim there is no future, other than the present it has sacralized. The transcript of the church affirms that nothing prevails over God as God moves through the poor, the obstruction of sin, and the arrival of a new future.

Another way to state the power and reality of grace is to affirm nothing is permanent but God: everything else is terminal. History is never fixed by those who presume to order it; it is opened up from beyond. The capacity to forgive evident in Jesus means the oppressed are empowered to resist false gods, nothing in the past is binding, and the future is liberated. A new order can and will arrive because of who God is, whose wounds are healing the distortions in history. When Martin Luther King stood at the Washington Monument and proclaimed, "Free at last, free at last, thank God Almighty, free at last" it was grace and forgiveness which made it possible.

As the church reclaims its words and controls their meaning, it becomes a rhetorical form of resistance to the rhetoric of the empire. And it renders the empire voiceless. By the Word, God called the creation into being, and by the Word of grace, God empowers a community to resist empire. Again, in the Epilogue consideration will be given to some concrete strategies about the role of the church in unmasking empire and leading the nation in new directions.

WORSHIP IN THE CONTEXT OF EMPIRE

CHAPTER FIVE

Introduction

In the life of the church, worship is the venue where the faith tradition contests the reality of empire, where the Gospel heritage discerns the penetration of imperialism in our national life, and in the very fabric of the church itself. Engagement with the God of the exodus and the God of the cross and resurrection is the most political event of our daily routine. This is not to contract the sphere of worship to the public arena or to dismiss the personal needs of the worshipers. But it is essentially a statement as well about our bearing in the world, especially a world defined by empire. In worship there is never less than an echo from empire that fills the public chambers and seeps into the church. It is not exempt from the ways in which empire penetrates the society and its institution.

Here one needs to make a distinction between worship as confirmation and worship as intervention. Worship as confirmation implicitly or explicitly sanctions the prevailing order. The most pernicious form is where the faith tradition gets wrapped around the flag. Patriotism and fidelity are intertwined. The national order is given divine authorization. The favoritism of ultimacy is continually advanced and the distinction between providence and foreign policy is dissolved. While Nazi Germany and the events of the Holocaust are tortuous memories of explicit sanctioning of an evil order, at a more subtle level one only has to reflect on some services before the 4th of July. Exceptionalism becomes a divine agenda. One could argue it is never appropriate to sing patriotic hymns in church. "My

Country Tis of Thee" is a problematic linkage. That suspends the tension between the faith tradition and the national formation as empire, or at least empire lite.

Worship as confirmation can take the form of silence, affirmation by default. It supports empire often by cloaking it in a religious blanket. Then worship advances the ideology that spirituality has an immaculate conception; it is uncontaminated by social, political, economic relations which shape our lives. It advances the internalization of a world defined by empire by its silence, retreats into a private enclave. When the arrangements of one's world are not addressed, the isolation of the faith authorizes it by its default. While the world is not celebrated, it is not acknowledged or challenged either. It makes a defining contribution to amnesia and thwarts the action of God in human history.

Worship as intervention creates an experience which at times is the most uncomfortable hour of a community's week. Far from being an escape from distress, it creates it as the world of the Gospel penetrates and unmasks the world of empire. Alasdair MacIntyre in *After Virtue* makes the point in generic terms. We should "not ask of a social institution: 'What end or purpose does it serve?' But rather 'of what conflicts is it the scene?'"[1] While the "struggles of the soul" have a place in worship and the life of the church, the soul has a context. And for our purposes the context is empire, the ways in which the nation is idolatrous, claiming for itself the power and authority to define reality for others as well as those within its sphere. Authentic worship, then, is where the power of God and the power of empire meet and contest authority. And it poses the question to the faith community, "To whom do you belong?" And, typically, it only has an hour to make the case for the God of exodus and resurrection.

The Identity of the Church
Some would say the church is the community that proclaims the resurrection; others would claim it is the community that lives it as

well. And when it lives the resurrection it is a political community
– but not a community of politicians! It may be difficult to imagine a
preacher being thrown into jail after his/her Easter sermon. But that
is precisely what is reported in the Scripture (Acts 4:1-3). Peter and
John stood by the God who brings life out of death and the empire
responded. In some ways the empire discerns the political nature
of the faith community more readily than some in that body. Those
who are threatened have their awareness focused. One has only to
consider the birth narrative of Jesus to document that; Herod knew
and responded to the challenge of "another King." The words over
the cross applied by the state also reflected Jesus' political nature.
"This is Jesus the King of the Jews" (Matthew 7:37).

When one thinks of the church as the community that lives the
resurrection, one needs to realize the ways in which the early church
envisioned it. It was both a future expectation and a present reality.
The event of raising Jesus from the dead is a message that includes
our ultimate destiny. And the validity of the faith tradition is at
the heart of the claim – "If Christ has not been raised, your faith is
futile..." (I Cor. 15:17). But the Hebrew Scripture and the Christian
Scripture converge in the affirmation of the power of God. Creation
and resurrection are one in the claim God creates out of nothing and
brings life out of death. "The God of resurrection, he (Tertullian)
reminds us is the all-powerful creator of life."[2] As such it is a present
reality to be lived. When one affirms that God defeated death, that
Easter morning cancels the Empire's victory on Friday, that goes
beyond a "heavenly enthronement" of Jesus.[3] The faithfulness of
God to God's promises prevails in this world as proclaimed. The
resurrection is a this-worldly event as well.

The church, then, is the community that lives the victory of
God in history. Death takes many forms, and empire is one of
them. Among other things the resurrection enables the courage to
confront the claims at odds with those of God. The God who brings
life out of death is engaged now in the world where idolatry and
injustice prevail. It was a resurrection moment in the famous kitchen

event when Martin Luther King lay down his head on the table, overwhelmed by the hate and forces of evil which threatened him and his family, and yielded to the power of God to prevail in this world. Secure in his ultimate destiny he was "raised" to the task of the civil rights journey. The resurrection is politically empowering and that is what the community of faith celebrates in worship

The resurrection is a political event and it sets forth a political mission. It gives rise to challenging empire in the confidence God is true to God's promises. It is agenda setting. The resurrection of Jesus is not just consoling but God's commissioning of us to live life and not death. Against the background of the Holocaust and his own internment in a prison camp for three years, Moltmann focused the cross and resurrection as "God's contradiction."[4] They lead to "unrest" and "impatience." Specifically, "those who hope in Christ can no longer put up with reality as it is, but begin to suffer under it, to contradict it. Peace with God means conflict with the world, for the goal of the promised future stabs inexorably into the flesh of every unfulfilled present."[5] When the community of faith engages in "passing the peace," it is not simply well-being but a determination to engage the world of death as God has and is a determination to divest any vestiges of imperialism and a stout determination to resist empire. Passing the peace is then, a resolve to break through the amnesia and embrace justice.

One thing that follows from this is that accommodation is preempted; alignment with the prevailing order is not an option. The seepage of death into the life and worship of the church is preempted. Those who live, the community of faith that lives the resurrection and is attached to God's agenda, cannot acquiesce to the empire. Everything about the community is fortified against it. When the church truly worships, the ties with the authority of the present order are severed. The worship sets the scene for contention, for resistance; it sets in motion a posture which not only cannot accommodate but aggressively purges the intrusion of empire into its life and its embodiment in the nation.

Rituals and Reality

We have been thinking about worship as the setting where conflicts emerge and worshipers are unsettled. Rituals play an integral role in the contest. Their creation and repetition establish the realities within which we live. We cannot really think of ourselves and our communities apart from rituals and what they create. In the final analysis, they are who we are.

Rituals are more than something recorded in a prayer book. Rituals create us and they create our sense of reality. When someone says "be realistic" the injunction is to correspond to some ritual created world. Tom Driver puts it bluntly: "If we did not ritualize, we would not speak. Ritualizing is our first language."[6] They enable us to understand our origins, imagine our destiny, and grasp who we are. While we may think we live in the realm of words, that realm has an origin and foundation. In a sense, we are enabled to "find our way" precisely because rituals enable that journey.

Rituals may be most evident, their significance far clearer, in situations of extremity. There we see their reality-creating function. And often what is drawn most starkly is competing senses of reality which rituals have created and sustained. Melissa Raphael enables us to see this in her book, *The Female Face of God in Auschwitz*. The routines established by the Nazi all contribute to the erasure of the Jews' humanity. These take the form of what is withdrawn as well as what is demanded. In this setting the significance of a tooth brush or a family picture looms exceeding large. The sleeping and "toilet" facilities, especially in the light of much dysentery, are debasing. The absence of tampons invades ones privacy. Then there are the routine line-ups and forms of accountability. These are compounded by prolonged and routine work functions. The designation by a tattooed number strips personhood of another marker of one's humanity. The rituals of the death camp tell you who you are, both in what they withdraw and what they require.

What is compelling about the reporting of Raphael is the counter-rituals creating a different reality. And while it's not exclusively among women in Auschwitz, it may have been most evident there. "Women's relationship with one another could set them apart from Auschwitz while still inside it; ...."[7] The rituals of care defied the degradation and dehumanization. While this often took the form of sharing a piece of bread or giving a source of warmth, the most distinctive rituals had to do with the face. Not looking away, but directly at another was a gift of humanity. The consolation of touch re-dignified another. And washing the face of another with the treasure of scarce water was restorative. All these forms of "relational sustainment"[8] were rituals that countered and sustained an identity the rituals of Nazis would erase. Women by ritual affirmed the divine image which the Nazis would expunge.

One of the things particularly compelling for our purposes is rituals contesting each other, and contesting the senses of reality they affirmed. We are apt to think of a ritual – as on Sunday morning – as being independent of the world and reality within which we live. This brings focus to our contention that worship, authentic worship, brings one world and its sense of reality up against another. The reality created by the exodus and cross/resurrection is competing with the rituals of empire and the reality it creates. Our rituals do not function in a vacuum. We are invented and sustained by rituals, so the question at hand is always "which ones."

What we need to be concerned with is ritual blending, letting symbolic actions co-exist as if compatible. Is a flag in the sanctuary defensible? Should essentially patriotic hymns be sung? Should sermons celebrate our national heritage? The answer might be "yes and no;" the issue is merging symbolic acts in such ways that there is ritual confusion at best and idolatry at worst. Worship should enable us to gain clarity on who we are, whose we are, and the nature of our journey.

We can gain some clarity on our theme by thinking directly about the two sacraments affirmed by Protestants – in divergent forms to be sure.

Baptism as Transferal

Baptism is a sacrament which enacts a transferal from the narrative of empire to the narrative of resurrection.

Unfortunately, the meaning of Baptism has been at best compromised. In one sense it has been designated as just one of those things you do with an infant – usually second only to vaccination! In another sense, it has become enshrined in ceremonial sentimentality. If not wonder-filled it has become a wonderful event. While the liturgy in varying degrees calls attention to a commitment to Jesus, the circumstantial setting takes on other meanings and dimensions. There is little resemblance to the biblical event. Think about it. Grandmother has created or at least purchased the baptismal gown. Mother is aglow but worried the child will wake up and cry – thus challenging her maternal capabilities. Father looks like he hasn't been in church lately. And with a mystical touch and glow, the Reverend moves through the congregation so all can adore the child. Individualism triumphs once again and a faith community focused on a crucified and risen Jesus has faded from consciousness. It all bears little resemblance to a baptismal dip in the river Jordon, dirt and seaweed ever present.

By contrast, baptism in its authenticity is defined by the resurrection. We have agreed with Madigan and Levenson: "In the ancient Christian churches, it was widely understood that the resurrection life could be anticipated and experienced before death. (And it) associated the beginning of this experience with the sacrament of baptism."[9] It marks the removal from one realm to another, from the life of one "reality" to another, deliverance from one domination to another allegiance. One anchor for the claim is John 3:5 which identifies baptism as a condition of entering the Kingdom of God. It is a transferal from a covenant of death to one of life. With baptism there is a fundamental rejection of one world and embrace of another. It marks a divide and a decision; one is "baptized into Christ Jesus" (Romans 6:30) and the resurrection life.

Baptism involves switching jurisdictions. It marks rejecting the claims of empire and living the realities it demands. In some liturgies this involves language like: "Do you renounce Satan?" That points to a determination to reject the claim which deters one from living the life in Christ. It would be a mistake to think of this in individual terms. For baptism takes place in a community, one that aspires to live the resurrection. Hence, it is an act of removal, either by parents who themselves have made a decision to whom they belong or the baptized one if beyond infancy. In either case, switching sides is the bottom line and the context is a community which knows which side of the divide it is on. And in baptism the Christian is welcomed. The divide is communal first and individual second.

Eucharist as Re-Centering
The celebration of the Lord's Supper is really the most blatant expression of contestation, or so it should be. Some Protestant traditions embrace it three or four times a year and one gets the sense, whether they need it or not. Other traditions practice it weekly and may not be sure why. At either extreme, it tends to be a ritual which provokes fellowship or yields assurance about ones destiny. Tom Driver notes the "the elements... have become mystical, privatized, and funereal."[10] That the event might have something to do with liberation from bondage is preempted. The anti-empire focus evaporates. It is hard to discern that the ritual has anything to do with social conditions and ones responsibility for them.

The Christian community seems to have obscured the fact that Jesus was a Jew and that the inaugural event was rooted in bondage and liberation. The upper room was a political statement in the fullest sense. Jesus was drawing a connection between the most important event in the life of Israel and his impending death and resurrection. The exodus from Egypt and the death/resurrection of Jesus are both about empire resistance. The power of God was in the journey from Egypt to a Promised Land and the power of God was evident on Easter morning. God has defeated the rulers of one's age. Our participation now is fundamentally a rehearsal even as it was that in the upper room. Once again, we celebrate "the anti-imperial origin of Israel."[11]

In a sense, one cannot bypass the Passover events to secure the Easter ones. If we do, we not only repudiate his Jewish reality but dissolve the Eucharist into some spiritual orgy secured by self-absorption. Think about what Jesus was celebrating on the night before the Friday/Sunday events. The Israelites were slaves, exploited in every imaginable way; they were flagrantly violated. The text reminds us that "the people of Israel groaned under their bondage and cried out for help..." And God said to Moses, "I have seen the affliction of my people... and I have heard their cry...I know their suffering, and I have come down to deliver them..." (Exodus 3:7). The ritual that night was a way of making present the God who stood up to empire and enabled the Israelites to claim their liberation. Jesus was centering his disciples on the power of God and linking his mission, ministry, and destiny to that power. In a sense he was saying, "This is that" or "that is this." He was invoking a "social memory."

When our practice of the Eucharist is defined by Jesus's inauguration of it in the midst of making present the God of the exodus, we can no longer reduce it to a spiritual spike. Fundamentally it is about living the resurrection now as well as proclaiming it as our destiny. The bread and the wine, defined by the empty cross, become more political than a rally or voting booth. In celebrating the death and resurrection (with the exodus in the foreground) we are acknowledging that God has defeated the empire and it is our mission to live that victory. Walter Brueggemann expresses it this way: "To participate in the Eucharist is to live inside the imagination of God,"[12] a vision of a world in which we are all liberated from the claims of empire. "Free at last" are the words that might be on our lips as we leave the table.

There is an intrinsic connection between the sacraments of Baptism and the Eucharist. The one is confirmation of the other, really. Baptism as transferal means at a given time a person is moved from one sphere of authority and reality to another. The Eucharist is a statement that we aspire to remain there. In baptism we are separated from the domain of empire and with the Eucharist declare our determination to live the resurrection and not the reality created by empire.

The Cross: Representation and Expectation

The cross is not a ritual; neither is it a sacrament. But it is at the center of both and defines them. Unfortunately, it has become decorative, a piece of polished brass rendered dysfunctional. What is obscured is the triumph of death and the power of the state to administer it. And the suspicion emerges that God was elsewhere at the time. When the cross of the first century no longer defines our sacraments, baptism becomes sentimental and the eucharist is reduced to a fellowship meal. In relation to the sacraments we need to recover "what the cross stands for" and "what it calls for." There is a necessary distinction but not necessarily a difference between the two. We can begin to penetrate this if we ask, "Who is on the cross?"

While there are those who focus on the suffering of Jesus on the cross – a recent movie grooves on that - Jürgen Moltmann refers to it as a "God event."[13] One could argue that one reason the cross for Protestants is empty is because there is no evident way to represent God as there. More than the resurrection defines the empty cross; the invisible God is on the cross; death has been included in God's inner reality. Moltmann goes on to say "…the meaning is that *this* is God, and God is like *this*. God is not greater than he is in this humiliation. God is not more glorious than he is in this self-surrender. God is not more powerful than he is in this helplessness. God is not more divine than he is in this humanity."[14] The cross is about more than Jesus; the depth of meaning in the cross is that we have a wounded

God. God did not take a pass on Golgotha.

From a Nazi prison camp Dietrich Bonheoffer wrote the now familiar words, "Only a suffering God can help."[15] In no other way can he be with us and for us. Only a love that suffers can make a difference. The God who allows himself to be crucified embraces our weakness and suffering and makes it God's own. Jesus was not like a letter as Church Fathers imagined – claiming that God was in Jesus in the sense a letter is in an envelope and can be withdrawn. Bonheoffer is claiming, God "stuck it out." At no other point was God so completely "in Christ" as on the cross. And in no other way can we be healed and restored.

What follows from seeing God as suffering on the cross, as affirming a suffering God, is that nothing broken in our lives is outside of God in any way. God is there. That means one can bring to the cross on the altar every hurtful frustration, the broken relationships that will not heal, the soldier in Iraq you pray is still alive, the guilt you cannot shake off, the secret struggles you never brought to words for another to hear. The suffering/crucified God is already in the midst of it. A wounded God is there and will not withdraw.

While this might seem remote to empire, in reality the suffering God is in all the consequences of its reign. Much, but not all to be sure, of the evil in the lives of many is a consequence of domination. The slaves working in the fields prior to the civil war understood that the God of Jesus was with them in their suffering and a part of it. And their survival and resistance was rooted in that presence. The cross on the altar in baptism and the eucharist makes clear who is there with us. And that is where love and hope are joined. As Moltmann again claims, this crucified/suffering God "consummates his unconditional love that is so full of hope."[16] The fact that love can be crucified is powerful and will overpower in humility/humiliation the power of the empire. When the sacraments are defined by the God on the cross, they constitute resistance to empire and the assurance of God prevailing.

The recognition of what the cross "stands for" leads into what it "calls for." The suffering God obligates; the crucified God claims us and is agenda-setting.

God is not alone on the cross. That God is there in Jesus surfaces those whom Jesus embraced. There is, according to Ignacio Ellacuria, a correlation between the crucified Jesus and the crucified people. "What is meant by 'crucified people' here is that collective body, which as the majority of humankind owes its situation of crucifixion to the way society is arranged and maintained by a minority that exercises its dominance through a series of factors...."[17] They are those who are victims of systemic arrangements which are created by the few and all to their benefit. Whether their condition is poverty and homelessness, oppression and humiliation, or hopelessness and despair, it is a function of worldly arrangements. In a sense, they are innocent victims in that their condition is not a function of any default on their part. Ellacuria is calling us to see them on the cross.

When we see them on the cross, it prompts us to ask "What have I done to crucify them?"[18] Their innocence does not extend to us. They suffer from systems from which we benefit. Our food excesses are theft from the hungry. Our freedom is often at the expense of their oppression. Their homelessness is a consequence of our domicile surpluses. Their crime infested neighborhoods are a function of our secure suburbs. Their imprisonment enables us to feel secure and comfortable. And the daunting reality is that God comes to us precisely in the "crucified people" who are usually invisible to us. Access to God is in solidarity with them and in resistance to the societal formations that create their condition. There is no access to God which is a detour around the "crucified people." In them the penetration of empire is most evident.

The suffering God calls us into the lives of those who are victims. And the question at the cross is, "What am I doing in order to uncrucify them? What ought I to do that this people will be raised?"[19]

Therefore, the cross at the communion table is a summons, a commitment generated to take the "crucified people" down from the cross. Here we need to remember that the community is involved in the sacrament, not simply an "I". Kneeling together before the cross on the altar, a community is committing itself to be at odds with the empire and come to the aid of those it victimizes. Participation in the sacrament defined by the "suffering God" is about personal transformation to be sure but explicitly a call to action in the world. It is the cross that keeps the Eucharist from being a pacifier for the future and a peace-engendering moment. The "crucified God" is there waiting impatiently to live in that reality and against that created by the empire. And there at the "ground beneath the cross" we can "no longer adapt oneself to society, its idols and taboos and (but) enter into solidarity with the victims of religion, society, and the state at the present day."[20] The cross politicizes the sacrament; it pits the "suffering God" against the realities empire has created and perpetrates.

Asking the question, "Who is on the cross" transforms the sacrament and blends the crucifixion of "the suffering God" with the obligation to serve the "crucified God" in the form of taking down from the cross "the crucified people."

What finally underwrites the political nature of the sacraments – and connecting them to empire and its resistance – is the radically political nature of the "Good Friday" event. The determination of the state to dominate and control reality finds definitive expression in the mode of Jesus termination. For this reason Moltmann claims "...the cross is the test of everything which deserves to be called Christian."[21] Crucifixion is the manner in which the state deals with those whom it considers subversive to its interests. And it is intended to send a message – even as the lynching of Blacks in America is intended to. Again, Moltmann reminds us that Jesus was crucified "basically in the name of the state gods of Rome who assured the *Pax Romana*." It was "not part of a general criminal jurisdiction."[22] Hence, the empire prevailed, or so it thought. One appendage to this contention centers on the role of Judas. He was not simply a frustrated follower venting disillusionment. The Gospel of John clarifies that Judas is "an agent of imperial power.... Judas comes for Jesus accompanied by a Roman cohort... and by officers from the high priests and Pharisees. The latter are apparently members of a temple security force...."[23] Mel Gibson's focus on "The Passion of Christ" is then an outrageous distraction from the political nature of the event as well as its theological focus on the suffering/crucified God.

Once we have a fix on the significance of the crucifixion in the light of the intentions of empire, the sacraments are politicized. Participation in them as a community is a declaration of which side we are on in the world and where our responsibilities lie. They enact a commitment to be with those the empire crucifies, and to "take them down from the cross." It is not easy to imagine anything that would make us more uncomfortable than that; and inner transformation needs to find form in a different world.

Worship defined by the exodus and the cross/resurrection of Jesus may create for the faith community the most uncomfortable hour of the week.

THE ECONOMY
AND EMPIRE
CHAPTER SIX

Introduction

Perhaps the most pervasive and persistent agent of empire is the economy. It is an institution uniquely equipped and adept at extending control beyond a country's borders. Capitalism has the aura of something sacred. Any critique of its ultimacy crosses over well established boundaries. In a very real sense, the market economy is who we are as Americans and it is self-legitimating. Over half a century ago, historian C. Van Woodward made the point unambiguously: "We (Americans) have showed a tendency to allow our whole cause, our traditional values, and our way of life to be identified with one economic institution. Some of us have also tended to identify the security of the country with the security of that institution ... we have showed a strong disposition to suppress criticism ... (and) have been tempted to define loyalty as conformity of thought ...."[1] The judiciousness of Woodward might well be tested by 9/11 and the Wall Street attack which some regarded as symbolic. It may be that one reason Americans resist the designation of empire is because it surfaces an institution we cannot imagine as problematic.

Given that reluctance, we will begin more cautiously by exploring ways in which several features of the ideology of capitalism are at odds with the faith tradition.

Ideology, Economics, and the Church

It was in 1958 that Karl Barth authored a controversial letter to a pastor in East Germany (*How to Serve God in a Marxist Land*). He had been asked to provide encouragement to those living under a Communist regime. Surely one who was unambiguously anti-Nazi would name the new totalitarian demon. But, he didn't! Barth turned the issue on end and said, "the real problem is serving God in the 'flesh pots of Egypt'!"[2] The economic order and gross materialism of the American reality were problematic. Barth argues there may be no freedom in a Communist land but in America freedom means you can dump corn in the sea while persons in the world die of hunger. While he recognized the tensions between Communism and the Gospel, "... godlessness in action ... is truly atheism."[3]

The letter which provoked some indignation in America for its unanticipated consequences focused on I Peter 5:8-9: "Be sober, be watchful. Your adversary the devil prowls around like a roaring lion, seeking someone to devour. Resist him, firm in your faith, knowing that the same experience of suffering is required of your brotherhood throughout the world." While Barth understood this text as emerging from the fact of "Christians living in a difficult situation,"[4] he did not proceed to name Communism as "the roaring lion" in ours. That equation he found simplistic and misleading. Indeed, it could be interpreted as a distraction. "For the real 'roaring lion,' ... may be much more difficult to distinguish, and the power of the adversary may well be at work in the West in less discernable forms."[5] That was the fatal flaw in the "Christian anti-Communist" movement here in the 60's and 70's. Because it knew where the devil was embodied in one grand act of totalitarianism it could not discern its emerging forms in our midst. Barth argues that naming Communism as the "lion" is to fall into the trap of "a dangerous optical illusion."[6] When resistance has a single target, naming the anti-Christ narrows the focus. The issue as Barth defines it is godlessness; whatever seduces us away from the Gospel tradition.

Communism may do that but for Barth the devil is more clever and industrious – and insidious as well. He takes many forms, many difficult to distinguish from our assumed values. Resistance needs to be equally discerning.

Walter Brueggemann articulates the theme of the enculturation of the American church and the loss of identity which ensues – or perhaps the loss of identity enables enculturation – and nails the issue to its institutional forms. The consequence is that the church has "little power to believe or to act."[7] While he identifies that enculturation as the "American ethos of consumerism" the underlying issue is starker. "Our consciousness has been claimed by false fields of perception and idolatrous systems of language and rhetoric."[8] Under the worst of circumstances, the underlying themes of Monday noon Rotary are echoed in Sunday morning services. To "suffer from amnesia"[9] is the plight of the faith community. Having forgotten the faith tradition the antithesis of it is advocated. In relation to the economic order the problem is that the outcome of market interaction is seen as neutral – neither good nor bad. But that masks the issues of poverty, homelessness, access to health care, all of which arise because the market institutions are keyed to respond only to price signals, and those supplant need with want.

Brueggemann makes a helpful distinction between the dominant and the alternative consciousness. The dominant consciousness is formed by the prevailing ideas and values and sustained by social institutions. It is the controlling way in which reality is conceived and perpetuated. The characteristic of this dominant culture Brueggemann describes as "grossly uncritical, (it) cannot tolerate serious and fundamental criticism, and will go to great lengths to stop it." It is what some refer to as "the real world," especially when parents think their children have gotten an overdose of college professors! The alternative consciousness has a different story, one shaped by the biblical tradition. And what it calls for is "a radical break with the social reality"[10] at hand. The business of the faith community for Brueggemann is to dismantle the false perception of reality and idolatrous systems. For Brueggemann the prophet is at the center of this process, awakening visions of a different reality grounded in the One he calls "the God of endings."[11]

One of the ways to foreground the issue of our social reality and its capacity to engulf the faith community is to invoke the concept of ideology. Both the dominant and alternative consciousness have one! Often, as not, ideology is used in a totally pejorative sense. Typically it is something to be avoided, a false consciousness which needs to be exorcised and replaced by something free of impurities! The concept is often invoked as a means of sustaining the prevailing order and dismissing its critics. They bring to the table a set of biases which inevitably distort their perceptions. Those with whom we disagree are ideological. Their lens is distorted; ours is not. Karl Barth did not use the term but his refusal to identify Communism as the enemy, the embodiment of evil, means he did not dismiss it as a uniquely false consciousness. An alternative is to lay claim to a more neutral understanding.[12] Everyone in a society has an ideology; it is the story we tell ourselves in order to interpret the vast quantity of information and images which our world sends us. We all have a perspective and it is socially based. An ideology is simply a point of view. And ideology can lead us to embrace the shared vision in our environment, accept it as valid and right. Or an ideology can enable us to be critical and imagine a world different from the one in which we are submerged. It gives us a picture of the world and creates institutions based on that picture. In the words of another scholar, "ideology refers to any pattern of concepts, theories, beliefs, and values... that link a human group together, interpret power relations ... and shape normative sensibilities."[13] Thus it can either secure or subvert the world in which we live. To refer back to Brueggemann, the dominant consciousness and the alternative consciousness are both steeped in ideology. And often the problem of the church and its message is that immersed in the values of the dominant order, it attaches them to the symbols of faith. As Peter Berger points out, "Religion legitimates effectively because it relates the precarious reality construction of empirical societies with ultimate reality."[14] One example of that was a journal called "Christian Economics." It was unadulterated Adam Smith. There you have an ideology steeped in self-interest curiously linked to a Gospel of neighbor-love. In the world construction of Brueggemann, theology and the economic order are competing ideologies. When enculturation occurs one ideology has voided the other.

There are at least three features of the economic ideology that clash with the theological one: individualism, the nature of freedom, and the nature of growth.

Certainly one core value of the economic order is the autonomous self. While individualism has some merit, the economy gives prominence to its dark side. And that comes in many shades but at base it is the assumption of the self as a rational agent pursuing his or her interests. President Bush has not likely steeped himself in economic theory but he represented a version of it in the summer of 2002. In the process of assuring the country that the worst was behind us he admonished, "Go out and spend some money." Better days can be assured if the individual consumes more. The individual as consumer is key and the necessary condition for the eventual benefit of all. And the accumulation of wealth by individuals is an unambiguous good thing; it enables more consumption.

But consider the dark side of this. What follows from the autonomous self seeking its own interest is the right of exclusion. What I earn and what I purchase is mine, singularly for my enjoyment. The desperation with which our American society affirms private property, and often sees it as a divine right, is one expression of the autonomous self. The sanctity of accumulated wealth in our society is beyond critique – by those who have it! Democracy always comes to a halt at the border of a trust fund. One student said she resented the fact that her parents' and grandparents' hard earned money paid in as tuition was used in part as financial aid for others. The irony was that she happened to be dyslexic and was very clear about the obligation of the academic community to provide her with services others did not need! The right of the autonomous self to privilege a need prevailed in one context but not another.

The alternative ideology is one that affirms being-in-community. The self has its authentic existence when seen in relationship, in solidarity with others. We are who we are in a web of connections and sustaining the web is a shared responsibility. The fundamental biblical categories are plural. The people of Israel and the Body of Christ are clearly corporate models of reality. There is really no autonomous self in the biblical tradition. Even transactions with God are finally not individual but communal. And self-love and neighbor-love are inextricably linked. The needs of the self and the needs of other selves are intertwined and inseparable. Nature is also an integral part of community.

It needs to be said that the individualism created and sustained by the economic order re-creates the Christian faith in its own image. Think, for example, of the ways in which spirituality has become a personal exercise. In former times some called it "manicuring the soul," gearing up for your salvation. And that has nothing to do with making the world more livable for others. The privatization of religion is a culmination of the autonomous self seeking its own interest. It is difficult to understand how some can find Jesus and not their neighbor. But it is an industry now. And when the faith tradition is sequestered in the private sphere it not only is subject to seepage but the ideologies of the public sphere go unchallenged. So the autonomous self reigns. Yet ironically, individuals are impotent in the presence of institutions like the economy. The autonomous self really has no power. It may nurture inner strength but in no sense can it pursue a social agenda.

A second element in the ideology fostered by the economy is the nature of freedom. In many ways this is a subset of the first point. One does not have to be an astute economist to recognize that the market values freedom, its own particular version of it. We get some sense of the dimension of this in the fact that "fifty-one of the world's one hundred largest economies are corporations."[15]

And the ideology which drives the success of these corporations is that "free trade" serves the prosperity from which all benefit. If in fact human beings are first and foremost animated by self-interest then the economy is best served by their getting "the most goods at the lowest cost."[16] We exist to consume and that lifts production and enhances profit – in the normal course of things. And normal means without external restraint.

Moe-Lobeda details how the economic game should be played according to assorted versions of neo-classical economics. First, no government interference. Individuals and nature will achieve wealth if the market is allowed to work. It is a complete system. Second, if countries or other bodies do what they do best the lowest cost will result and all will benefit. Specialization without reference to its consequences is the agenda. There is a "comparative advantage" in specialization. Finally, in a free market there is equal power in the trading powers. Competition at every level, unfettered competition, will stand guard against exploitation.[17] When the market is allowed to work there will be "competitive prices, free choice, efficiency, economic growth, and maximum profit for producers."[18] It really is a perfect world if left to function on its own!

But the demon in this analysis is a notion of freedom uninhibited by accountability. It reminds one of the impulses behind the Kipling poem – the poet referred to going to the Panama Canal where there are no Ten Commandments – no restraints and you answer to no one. There is no doubt that it works – if by work one means that wealth-formation is the target. And those who live this creed are clear that if flaws emerge in the outcome the system is OK; only individuals get out of line. Not all are willing to contend that the poor are lazy but the ideology of freedom without restraint still prevails. It's tiresome to refer to past scandals but former President G. W. Bush said there are only a few rotten apples and initially was reluctant to embrace systemic change. Interference remains the prevailing sin. When fifty-one of the one hundred largest economies are corporations functioning on the agenda of free trade, one begins to see that we are only talking about freedom for some! Over a decade ago Cobb and Daly summed it up this way; "The world that economic theory normally pictures is one in which individuals all seek their own good and are indifferent to the success or failure of others engaged in the same activity."[19] Thus, the bumper sticker, "Whoever dies with the most toys wins." Here is a view of freedom that assumes "we are not constituted by our relationships but are separate entities free to pursue self-interest." If it happens that "GE brings good things to life" it is a result of "an unplanned coincidence of interests rather than a commitment to social well-being."[20]

Our concern is that freedom without restraint leads to restraint without freedom.[21] The accumulation of economic wealth that is the goal of the self-interested individual leads inevitably to the accumulation of power, and unrestrained power clearly limits freedom. That contrasts with the triangular relationships of self-God-and-neighbor. True freedom is in a covenant, in connections and commitments. Concurrent with history there is always an element of freedom. And systems like the market can magnify that exponentially. There is a difference between free markets and the freedom in Christ. God and the neighbor are boundaries within which our freedom is enacted. A market without God "enables it to exclude those most in need, enshrine privilege, and assign to itself the qualities of ultimacy. The presence of God in the market would challenge privilege, reveal domination, and preclude carelessness. What the reality of God does in relation to the market is make the necessary condition for human livelihood nonnegotiable for those conditions are defined by the work of the divine in human history."[22]

Douglas Meeks wrote some years ago that the church can speak to almost any issue of social justice except ones lodged in the economy.[23] While there might be a number of reasons for that, certainly one is the market notion of freedom. It does not rise to the level of a homiletical agenda. Only a most unusual faith community would engage the notion that freedom can be insidious. Most clergy and certainly their congregations are ill-equipped to tackle the issues of a free market because they have bought into it. They do not recognize that the freedom to make others poor and oppressed is alien to the biblical tradition. The "axis of evil" is structural rather than dispositional and their religion is lodged in the private and personal spheres.

A third feature of the economic ideology follows from the first two and it is the nature of growth. The prominence of that in our thinking makes it an unlikely target for criticism. How could any rational being be against it? More goods for more people has to be desirable! But the market has a version of growth that is problematic. It assumes that consumption is inherently a social good; everyone benefits when there is more productivity and consumption. One could almost suggest that there is now an eleventh commandment. Social well-being is enhanced with the more I buy, the more I replace, and with the exaggeration of my needs others are given employment. All benefit from my consumptive life style. At the very least, strong consumer spending makes the stock market go up. But the ability to pay is a condition for meeting needs. A starving family needs food but that does not register with our existing economic system.

It is patently obvious that the ideology of the market plays on needs as the pathway to growth. Douglas Meeks even suggests that needs take the place of God-talk.[24] They are alleged to be at the core of our being, the essence of what it means to be human. I need therefore I am! Recently an eleven-year-old daughter put it on the line with her Mother. "I need cosmetics, a cell phone, and a boyfriend." The Mother was most startled by the boyfriend! The eleven year old is only reflecting her society with the assumption that the creation and satisfaction of needs is the path to the good life – for ourselves and therefore others in the wake of our satisfaction of them. And the irony is that the more needs we satisfy the less satisfying they become! Satisfaction diminishes as needs are exploited. Finally, the outcome is the commodification of life; I am what I own – we become grand acquisitioners! And a healthy economy demands that.

But growth can be re-defined. Again, Douglas Meeks sets the contrast of ideologies. "Growth should not be based on infinite needs and acquisitions leading to an ever-widening appropriation of nature for the sake of accumulation of wealth as power. Rather, growth should be a deepening of human capacities for service of human development within community."[25] In a small Ohio village one Church started the Habitat for Humanity initiative in the area and with others built nine houses. Then the Church Board resolved to raise the money and build a house with their own people. On a fine spring day its members met outside the Church to celebrate their commitment. As they did that, some happened to look across the street at another Church. They were having a ground breaking for a 1.5 million dollar addition to their new addition! With all apologies for being like the Elder Brother, and the Pharisees saying, "I thank you God that we are not as other churches" – there are two alternative models of growth. It is fair to claim that the economic model of growth triumphs in many churches and members feel impotent to put a brake on it.

Whenever an ideology has taken hold in a society defining its sense of reality, one cannot avoid the feeling of inevitability. In the measure we hear the voice of an alternative consciousness, it seems weak and impotent. On the one hand, as Christians we are committed to the ideology of neighbor-love grounded in the Jesus event. And on the other we may come to realize that "we find ourselves in an ungodly situation, locked into a global political economy that structures exploitation into the very fabric of our lives."[26] Children in the world die of hunger because of the food and clothing produced for our use of land and in factories that should serve their own needs.

Chandra Muzaffar contends, "that the unjust global economy and the greed inherent in it can only be 'subverted' through a profound transformation of the self."[27] And that does not occur by virtue of teaching or simplistic faith affirmations but "through playful entertaining of another scripting of reality that may subvert the old text... and lead to the embrace of an alternative text and its redescription of reality." The Baptismal font and the Lord's Table can be where the dominant consciousness is subverted and the "redescription of reality" happens.[28] But that is the argument of another chapter.

Empire and The Market

Ideological stress is not as threatening as surfacing the market in capitalism for critical analysis. There "a strong disposition to suppress criticism"[29] kicks in and charges of being un-American seep into the conversation. In addition to being unpatriotic, it is difficult to imagine an economic system for America which does not pivot in some measure on the reality and necessity of a market for the production and distribution of goods and services. And one does not necessarily have to. The issue may be not the existence of a market but the ways in which it is envisioned and what drives it.

It is not difficult to document the claims that there are those – individuals and nations – whom the market disadvantages and traps. Globally, one can note that 1.3 million people have daily incomes of less than a dollar a day. One in five persons live in debilitating poverty from which they are unlikely to ever emerge. In America the disparity between unemployment rates for black vs. white teenagers is substantial and is exacerbated in times of economic stress (consider the 2009 recession). Women and men of comparable ability experience wage differentials which are unjustifiable. The litany is relentless. While the market can be said to have failed, it does not necessarily follow it is inherently evil.

The problem emerges initially when persons think of it as inherently good. At its outer limits this can take both a secular and a religious form. One can think of economists from Adam Smith to Milton Friedman who believed in the market as a complete system which values freedom. Free markets and freedom itself are coordinates. Eventually, the good of all is secured by a market free of interferences. At its best it is utopia. But the more serious issue surfaces in a religious frame work. Michael Novak, who is the house theologian at The American Enterprise Institute, argues that the capitalist market system is the incarnation of the Kingdom of God in history.[30] Somehow, by the work of the Holy Spirit, the divine reality became embodied in the free enterprise system and therefore is authorized from on high. Inevitably, its innocence is self-evident and it transcends critique. When the market has become a sanctuary the only appropriate role is to enter the holy of holies. One might find Novak dismissible but the issue may be one we have considered earlier – the secular becomes religious. Then it is really uncontestable.

In any case, a relentless impotence results for any person seeking alternation or modification. "In absolutizing the market, in assuming the market's logic as something omnipotent, capable of producing supra-human results, against which we should not show any resistance…" forecloses the possibility of addressing issues of apparent exclusion.[31] It is beginning to sound like paradise, or at least the promised land. Whether or not one envisions an "invisible hand," the efficiency and expediency of the market are threatened by any tampering with it. Thus, a "cruel mystique"[32] hovers over the market and precludes resistance. Once absolutized, its laws take on a sacred aura. When empire takes the form of dominance, then a sacralized market is its agent.

We have been contending that the church has a significant role in relation to empire and this is again an opportunity for resistance. In relation to the market, the church has at least three possible responses. The first is to hold up those for whom the market does not work and affirm their relative innocence. Economic considerations need to begin with those excluded from its benefits rather than economic laws. They need to be relativized! While the market thrives on the accumulation of wealth it needs to address the reduction of poverty. The measure of a system is, whom it fails before whom it benefits. At whose expense does accumulation take place? Wealth need not be seen as inherently evil. But, if it is "a theft from the poor" in some authentic sense, it needs to be called to account. Self-interest needs to be subordinated to the needs for livelihood of all. In short, "…the economy must exist for the life of all people rather than people existing for economic laws based on the accumulation of wealth."[33]

Needless to say, the market does not gravitate to those marginalized by it. But that does not mean an institution like the church – with others – can't demand its attention.

A second form of intervention focuses on the reality of what is really Transcendent. Once the market has been set apart, it is essentially endowed with transcendent qualities. The market becomes transcendentalized. Absolutization not only puts it beyond critical analysis but becomes that which one serves and in some sense worships. It becomes an altar around which mortals center their existence. In fact, they become commodities whose usefulness in the system defines worth. In simplest terms, the market has been idolatrized. Few would overtly think of it as God but that does not conceal the reality it functions as an ultimate. And what one sees as ultimate is defining for person's institutions and systems. The role of the church is to unmask the false transcendent. It is the community that witnesses to who God is and the only authentic incarnation, Jesus, the risen one. "The best way of denying the transcendentalization of the market that sacrifices the poor is to witness that God, even while present in the world, is not identified with the world or with any other institution, because God is wholly transcendent."[34] This affirmation renders blasphemous that claim of Michael Novak that the economic system is the embodiment of the Kingdom of God. And it is not less decisive in unmasking any claims that the market is the willing agent of freedom and human fulfillment. At some point accumulation becomes a sin in that it is organized against the One who came to bring life not death. Indeed, a transcendentalized market is an agent of death. In the measure the church witnesses to the God of Jesus Christ, it relativizes the market and summons it to function for those at the margins.

A third form of intervention concerns the transformation of desire. At the end of the previous section we referred to a new scripting of reality enabling a "transformation of the self." What the market generates, authorizes, and legitimates is a fundamental desire and the power which results. Accumulation is anything but innocent and benign. It may be a necessary evil; capitalism would not function without it. In a sense, the Fall is evident in it as well as the desire generates insensitivity. We noted earlier that the autonomous self is a central piece in the ideology of the market economy. The desire for having makes the market work for some – and not others. And a self-centered self drives the system. Now self-regard in some degree is necessary; it is integral to loving others. But the message of the church is that the self is inseparable from other selves; we are not separate units but in a profound sense overlap. Separation is what marginalizes them and what diminishes their humanity. A necessary correlate of desire is solidarity and that modifies it dramatically. The faith community sustains an environment in which others "may have life, and have it abundantly," John 10:10. The issue then becomes, desire at whose expense? The inseparability of individual selves with the selfhood of others is at the heart of the Gospel. The neighbor in need is a boundary that modifies accumulation. In the measure desire is transformed, it becomes life-giving rather than death-giving. It may not bring the market to a halt but it will cause it to serve the well-being of all. Again, Sung clarifies the issue: "Salvation comes through the pursuit of eating, drinking, clothing, housing, health, freedom, affection, and acceptance for the little ones, for those excluded by society, those who cannot pay us back or reciprocate."[35]

It is the mission of the church – in consort with other institutions – to mentor the market so that it becomes life-giving rather than death-dealing. And in doing that, the cruel insensitivity of empire is resisted.

Empire and Globalization

Once globalization is factored in, the reach and consequences of the economy become more stark.In the broadest sense, one might think of globalization as "the worldwide diffusion of practices, expansions of relations across continents, organization of social life on a global scale, and growth of a shared global consciousness."[36] At its best it is a universalizing which enables a "scripting of reality" in the interest of political, social, economic and cultural commonality. The outcome is a world in which there are common values and accommodating institutions. Insularity is overcome. While its critics are concerned with homogenization, its advocates accent communication and shared interest. Globalization leads to a new world in which the divisions of an old world are transcended. What is promiscuous is when one nation has the power and the will to impose its "scripting of reality" in all its manifestations. Then the freedom, which is an alleged outcome, is compromised if not fatally wounded. The slave is free to live in the world the master has created. Globalization is, then, an agent of empire; whomever has the power to impose its sense of order and export its institutions is the global master. It can lead to a more friendly world or a more oppressive one.

Our concern here is economic globalization, the ability to establish a system of exchange which does not inevitably benefit all. One could think of it simply as exporting capitalism, the effect of which can maximize exclusion. In the measure that it is driven by the accumulation of wealth, the life of all people is sacrificed. Economic globalization is a market economy writ large with all the possible enrichments and inevitable inequalities. The rhythm of the system enables the concentration of accumulated wealth to prevail. The management of scarcity is in the hands of the few. Hence, a globalized economy has the capacity to disable democracy. It "subordinates democratic political power to unaccountable economic power."[37] In a world of victors, victims no longer have the means to shape society in their interest. Then the economy is life-threatening for the poor. The economy becomes a form of terror.

And agency is disabled.

Again, this is not to argue that a market economy is inherently evil. It is predisposed to it, and especially when it is an agent of empire.

While the individual is left feeling helpless and is – when the economic system serves the interests of the few – the church as an institution is not. Given the crucified and resurrected Christ, everything is relativized. The staying power of every worldly entity is finally eroded; nothing can prevail. As we have argued previously, that is the foundation of the church. It is the resurrection community which lives in the reality of a victory in history. But, more particularly, it is the message of the church which counters and ultimately defeats human constructions of reality. It centers on Jesus "total faithfulness to the mission he received from God of announcing the radical dignity of all human beings..."[38] And it takes the concrete form of the coming Kingdom of God, the Reign of God that never fully fits in this world, but serves to transform it. That message forms a human community whose existence is rooted in a determination to create a just order in the world. That trumps the accumulation of wealth as a transcending goal of the economy. The church joins and embodies institutionally God's work in the world "to feed the hungry, heal the sick, visit the prisoners...." Wealth accumulation in some measure is not inherently evil – unless it is at the expense of the poor and creates victims. Economic victimization may seem impenetrable, but there is another script. The church is the community that aspires to live the script and command the market to serve social justice. "Global capitalism can be changed and redirected by human decisions...."[39] And that decision within a community is to live into the world God promises and not the one empire advocates and imposes. The reign of God contests globalization.

The economy need not be an agent of empire; it can be driven by the message of the Reign of God.

COMMODIFICATION
AND COMMUNITY

CHAPTER SEVEN

Introduction

Empire willingly and willfully engages in commodification. Its agenda is to transform whatever it approaches and desires into usefulness for its purposes. Without regard for any intrinsic value, empire converts into things whatever it aspires to control because things can be easily bought and sold. Empire has no tolerance for intrinsic value except as an object serving its agenda. To fashion a word, commodification is "thingification." Hence, it is inherently exploitive. By contrast, community enters into relationships and partnerships. At its best, it affirms and sustains the value and worth of what it embraces. Ownership and possession are not marked by control and usefulness. For empire, the public transcript is commodification. For the church, the hidden transcript is community.

The distinction is particularly stark in relation to economics. For example, in empire ownership is absolute. Possession of property is without compromise or qualification. The claim is absolute, whether it is food, land or a mode of production. It is mine and I have jurisdiction without regard to others needs or desires. Grain can rot in my silos while others die of starvation. Whatever value there is to the grain is a function of whatever use I may choose to make of it. Rights are exclusive and inalienable. Self-possession is necessary and legitimate. In the framework of community, property is not simply an entity. It is a social good and has a social purpose.

As noted earlier, Kathryn Tanner in *Economy of Grace* has a different take from empire. She asks, "What if God simply gives us what we need in an utterly gracious way and expects us to organize our lives with one another accordingly?"[1] God then becomes the norm for property and for sharing with others. The well-being of all becomes the standard that modifies ownership. Property exists in relationships, not independent of them. Neither the neighbor in need nor properties are commodities.

As we considered in the section on exceptionalism, empire affirms the right and even obligation to impose its values, will, and institutions on others – allegedly for their good as well. There is no sense of community and shared interests. Empire can extend its "good" to others in contempt for what exists in another community in terms of values or institutions. When commodification is the accepted agenda, imposition without regard for the interests of others is legitimate and necessary. Whatever is "there" is an obstacle to be removed or transformed.

For the church, the Trinity serves as a norm, a lens through which one grasps reality. The persons of the Trinity are distinct but inseparable. Solidarity not self-interest is the norm. "The persons of the Trinity therefore only give to one another what they have and hold in common."[2] There is no singularity of interests or intentions. And what the Trinity calls for in community is institutions and values of mutual benefit. To be specific, Tanner says the rich "should consider the poverty that others suffer to be something that is happening to them."[3] The church is called to be both a community of mutual benefit and one that struggles to organize the world for mutual benefit. Commodification is not an option. For the church, de-commodification is inherent in its Trinitarian understanding of God.

Religion and De-Commodification

Empire and the church compete for producing a world that establishes itself as objective reality. They each engage in a process of social formation which has profound consequences. And while empire, as we have argued, engages in commodification, the hidden transcript of the church is one of de-commodification. The perception of personhood is radically different. While both aspire to order experience, they differ radically in the nature of the self which exists in their reality. For empire the self is commodified and therefore a victim of intentions outside of it. Frederick Herzog draws a significant distinction between the "private self" and the "corporate self."[4] The private self is centered in itself; it is free of lateral engagement and responsibility. While it may appear to withdraw from the public arena, in fact it is subject to the determination of external realities; in this instance, it serves the interests of empire. It is in its apparent interest to do that. It may or may not really have a choice. Empire controls in the broader sense but it also commodifies the individual self so that it is an object in its agenda. By contrast, the self in the reality of the church is a corporate self. While in some sense singular, at core it is inclusive and committed to solidarity. Within the corporate model, a self is distinguishable but cannot disassociate itself from others. That which on the surface is not me, is in reality part of me. In this sense it reflects the Trinity as interpreted in a previous chapter. The English language does not lend itself readily to the distinctions between selves. Boyong Lee helps articulate this with reference to the Asian language.[5] In that discourse, I-ness language yields to we-ness language. When referencing I, my, and mine the word *uri* is used and really means our. Nothing exists in singularity. This is also evident in Japanese linguistics. The word *jibun* denotes a self that is inseparable from other selves. To wit, "oneself is an inseparable part of ourselves."[6] The boundaries of the self include a social whole. To return to Herzog, the "corporate self" embraces while the "private self" narrows the boundaries of self to oneself.

To accomplish its goals, empire aspires to create a world of disconnected but obedient selves who become ready agents of its agenda. The self within its own boundaries is susceptible to victimization. And the victim is bereft of lateral connections or obligations. If one thinks back to World War II and the isolation inflicted on American prisoners by the Japanese, we can see how isolation enabled the capturers to control individual prisoners and eventually lead some to betray the interests of their comrades. Deprived of contact with others, the disconnection with them become total. One could note the same phenomenon in the death camps created by the Nazis. Every effort was made to set off the individual self so that it had no sense of connection with others. Their interests and needs were dissipated. Empire does that on a large scale. The task or role of the church, then, is to re-establish the corporate self where I-ness has been transformed into we-ness. It is the "body of Christ" not a collection of individuals. Solidarity not singularity prevails in community.

Herzog has an important interpretation of the passage in John 3:1-21 where the issue of being born again appears.[7] Conservatives have traditionally reduced that narrative to, "Have you found Jesus?" The individual is set apart and privatized. Herzog centers on, "Have you found your neighbor?" De-privatization occurs in community. To be born again is to enter into a new relationship with oneself, one that is corporate and in solidarity with others, especially the powerless and poor. And it is a selfhood with open borders. The core of ones being is in solidarity with the beings of others. There is in the process of being born again, a new identity, a new selfhood, one in which one can distinguish oneself from others but not disassociate from them. The borders of the self are flung open and exclusion is not an option.

The public transcript of the empire is one that depends on creating and sustaining a "private self." It can work its will when self-encapsulation prevails. But the hidden transcript of the church enables resistance and rebellion. It centers on the creation of a community where human well-being is defining and the interests of all are included. Inclusion thwarts the agenda of empire. The very ways in which the church de-commodifies the self equips the community to stand apart and stand against. And that is a threat to the agenda of empire.

Welcome and Embrace in Community

Empire commodifies the self; it renders it an object to be exploited. Community engages in de-commodification. It's a context in which the agency of another is sustained. To be born again is to have a selfhood without the burden of self-interest. The other self is welcomed rather than used. Letty M. Russell references the analysis of Musa Dube in relation to the agenda of empire. "She understands imperialism to be a structured imposition of a few standards on a universal scale that assumes the 'others' is a blank slate to be (1) inscribed with a universal (Western) culture in disregard of their own particular culture, and (2) rendered dependent on those who maintain these standards."[8] And the range of issues and forms of control are without boundaries. Dominion over is the connection of choice. Imposition is an honorable mode. Control is absolute.

Drawing again upon the Trinity, the hidden transcript of the church focuses on partnership rather than privilege. The mode of existence is inclusive rather than exclusive. In an earlier chapter we incorporated the legitimation of the American empire in *The Case for Goliath* by Michael Mandelbaum. He contends that everyone benefits when the gorilla keeps things in order; world government is an art form and America has perfected it. What is currently missing is any of the issues of exclusion and social injustice which prevail in America and are ignored in the global sphere. Mandelbaum's professed commitment to peace, democracy, and free markets manages to overlook those who are not benefiting from them. One searches the text in vain for references to gender, race, classism and poverty. The dialectic of rich and poor, oppressor and oppressed, victimizer and victims seem to be off his chart. And they are off the agenda of empire for which domination is an inherent goal in global politics and economics. Apparently, order without justice is a tolerable trade-off. Those who are excluded, are excluded! Commodification has canceled community, partnership, and meaningful forms of inclusion. There is no effort to think from the margins, to open the borders of selfhood to include the needs of others. Clearly free markets have not taken care of that and democracy is subverted.

The "hidden transcript" of the church includes the recognition that God's wrath is visited upon the instruments of exclusion. God is intolerant!! When people are no longer included in the benefits of the society, then those structures of alienation must have their power challenged and defeated. One need only reference the episode in Genesis (11:1-9) concerning the tower of Babel. The construction of a tower to reach the heavens and thus consolidate power and control is met by the fall of the nations. The human construction of reality is thwarted. Unity and uniformity are at odds and are irreconcilable. The people are scattered by God and confusion accompanies their language. Domination will not prevail in the economy of God. And the church is the community with that article of faith and that mission.

But, the other side of that is the welcoming or embracing of other selves, especially those who are victims of the realities from which the few benefit. Control is a forfeited agenda in community. As the church focuses on the Trinity for its sense of reality, the consequences of exclusion can only be understood as a violation of God's presence in history and God's management of the household. Michael E. Lee quotes Gustavo Gutierrez's assertion that "without justice there is no salvation."[9] In the faith community, no one is outside the border because of who and where God is. Inclusion of the stranger is the agenda and the reality that God wills and works toward. Someone noted that the injunctions to love the neighbor appear once in Scripture but love of the stranger thirty times. Horsley notes that there is *one* legitimate exclusion. "The kingdom of God that brings renewal for the people, however, utterly excludes the people's rulers and places them under God's judgment."[10] Well-being in community and the structures it creates are at the head of the hidden transcript. Welcoming the stranger means embracing her/his pain, solidarity with her/his struggle for justice, and confidence that the presence of God's present God-self is with the victimized. Welcoming and embracing are in partnership with the Divine in history.

The transcript of the empire is marked by fear and that of the church marked by hope. The contrast is stark. Empire achieves its purposes through intimidation. As it commodifies, it claims a utopia at the expense of selfhood and personhood. And fear surrounds the claim its domination will be challenged. The hidden transcript unmasks the grounds of fear and names them as grounded in idolatry. And it surfaces the hope grounded in a God whose presence in history is on behalf of those left out. The faith community de-commodifies and opens the future to the purposes of One who prevails without domination, but love.

Jack Nelson-Pallmeyer notes there is a profound difference between empire and a republic. In an empire the interests of a powerful few prevail. It subverts on a global scale the priorities of others. An empire inflicts its will while a "republic is concerned with the well-being of all its citizens ..."[11] and does so in the context of the community of nations. Its inclusion is marked by partnership. Republic is a political reflection of the community evident in the church. And it is what the church aspires to nurture in the public sphere.

The Exodus Church

Another contrast between empire and the church is that the first is a cult of the absolute while the other is the cult of co-humanity. Once again, commodification and community are at odds. As we have argued, empire has no sense of ambiguity in relation to its intentions. What it envisions as good is good for all without qualifications. Community by contrast is marked by the well-being of all over time. And it resists commodification. This raises the question, "What is it about the church as a community that can withstand the pressure of empire? Why doesn't the church accommodate to the prevailing disorder?" Of course, it can and it has yielded; but it also has a history of resistance. What image of the church as community serves to sustain its commitment to co-humanity, the well-being of all? Connecting it to the exodus event is transformative.

In the 13th chapter of Hebrews, the author invokes a series of obligations for the community. "Do not neglect to show hospitality to strangers... Remember those who are in prison... Keep your life free from the love of money... Do not be lead away by diverse and strange teaching... So Jesus also suffered outside the gate... Therefore let us go forth to him outside the camp..." Then comes the condition that makes the difference: "For we have no lasting city, but we seek a city which is to come" (Hebrews 13:1-13). From the text Jürgen Moltmann names the church the exodus community and Christianity consequently focuses on a "pilgrim people of God."[12] Accommodation is not an option. The community can never settle in and settle down. It is always focused on "a city which is to come." While it functions in an environment where the cult of absolute prevails, and persons are commodified, its agenda is one of co-humanity. The church cannot venerate whatever is at hand because it is lead by its relation to God. To think of an exodus church is to surface the memory of a people who were at the mercy of the Egyptians but were lead by One who was ahead of them in the clouds. With that legacy, the church is a pilgrim people who resist the opportunities to solidify their position by accommodation and find a driving force in the One who is a head of them. In this sense it is always "socially irrelevant" and stands "in the social no-man's land" faithful to "transcendent determination of co-humanity as community."[13] Then the church is a community marked by "constant unrest" and "resist(s) the institutionalized stabilizing of all things."[14] It becomes immunized against the purposes of empire.

The church, then, is the community which lives from a horizon, a horizon defined by the Christ event. "It is open for the 'future' which comes to pass *in* it, yet in its *coming to pass* is recognized to be still *outstanding*."[15] It is never fulfilled but lives by hope and expectation. What Moltmann calls the power of the future, an arriving future, drives its reality. It meets the agents of fear with the promise of hope. It lives in opposition and in resistance. But one issue for many, is the role of those who in the fullest sense are not oppressed or oppressors, who are neither the Egyptians nor the Israelites. How do middle class persons and a middle class church find their place in a polarized narrative, a binary scenario with either Pharaoh or Moses? Laurel A. Dykstra identifies one option. As individuals and as a community, can we see ourselves as Miriam? Pharaoh's daughter lives in the privilege of the empire but does not submit to its agenda. She "is a decisive actor. She works together with other women despite differences in class, nation, and age; she forms alliances."[16] Miriam takes the slave child, Moses, into the palace and enables his Mother to be his nurse. "In the cosmic struggle Pharaoh's daughter takes sides."[17] Inside the palace she conspires and collaborates with other women to enable the Israelite to grow into the role God appointed for him. In time, Moses will lead his people to freedom in a promised land. It would not have happened without Miriam. "A woman of rank, privilege, and power, in a crisis situation, listens to perhaps the least powerful person she is likely to encounter: the female child of a slave (Moses' sister). And she allows the child to offer the plan, to tell her what to do, to listen and to be directed by the least may be the beginning of our journey out of Egypt."[18] That is the way of salvation open to the church. Because of her interference, Moses was not thrown into the river as decreed by her Father and his Mother became his nurse. Thus she is an agent of co-humanity which subverts the agenda of the empire and the cult of absolute.

When the church sees itself as an exodus community it cannot settle in and accommodate to the forces of empire. It stands apart from and in resistance to the "existing disorder." With Miriam it can embrace humanity and solidarity with the weak and helpless and live toward a future which is in the process of coming. Community subverts commodification and the cult of absolute. Community welcomes and embraces the stranger as it waits for what is to come, even as it is present in a measure.

JAMES CONE:
A THEOLOGY OF RESISTANCE
CHAPTER EIGHT

Introduction

James Cone does not use the language of empire. He could have. If his earlier work had been in the 21st century, he might have. Slavery and the history of oppression, continuing even now, is a devastating example of domination within American borders. And it is a violation at every level and at every time of some of the nation's professed values. The silence of the American church has been pronounced. As we noted earlier, the lynching of blacks after church and for entertainment at picnics is a stark, unforgiveable memory. Two events in the summer of 2009 are blunt reminders that racism is not dead in America. While the level of hate represented by the intruder in the Holocaust museum might seem to be singularly directed at Jews, the reality is that a black guard was assassinated in the entry. He was disposable in the pursuit of anti-Semitism. The second event was the closing of a swimming pool to black youths in Philadelphia. One irony was that the black daughters of the American President were greeted enthusiastically across the globe, while at the same time they could not swim at the club in America.

The history of slavery in America is decisively related to empire. Stephen D. Moore notes that "Empire and torture tend to be integrally intertwined... not to have one's own physical person at ones disposal..." is the depth of it.[1] The owning of another human being only begins to secure the depth of exploitation. The ability of slave owners to use a young black girl for pleasure, to separate a wife and children for profit, to whip uppity ones as examples to others, to transport Africans in slave ships, and to daily degrade blacks in work settings, all are evidence of empire. It would be a mistake to assign racism to the past. Emilie M. Townes writes, "Empire is part of black church life ... (white legislators) pass domestic spending cuts that eat the heart out of education, child care, access to health care and affordable healthcare, social security and Medicaid and Medicare and radicalize drug laws..."[2] Racism may be more subtle in the twenty-first century but its shrill dehumanization is no less real. And this victimization by whites raises profound theological issues, especially in relation to God. James Cone's theology of liberation serves as a model to the whole church of doing theology from below, from the victims and the marginalized.

God and Resistance

For James Cone, the God who neither slumbers nor sleeps is not up for debate. Up-front he writes, "the reality of God is presupposed in Black Theology... (The issue becomes) what we can say about the nature of God in view of God's self-disclosure in the biblical history and the oppressed condition of black America."[3] As we will see, Cone is clear about the divine activity; what is at issue is the structure and institutions of the nation, and the church in particular. Cone names oppression as the correlate of God's liberating work. Slavery and oppression can be thought of as epoch-making events but they in no way block access to God. The black struggle for freedom is not only compatible with the God of Scripture but is a reification of that God. What God did once in Egypt is "identical with the liberation of the weak and poor" now.[4] That claim is integral and defining for the church and its mission.

Cone does not use the language of "root experiences" but one can argue that there are two for Black Theology, the exodus and the Christ event. "By delivering this people from Egyptian bondage and inaugurating the covenant on the basis of that historical event,

God is revealed as the God of the oppressed, involved in their history, liberating them from human bondage."[5] Cone sees this to be historical in the most radical sense. This becomes most clear when he claims that liberation is the content of salvation. The initiation of a covenant with an oppressed people is significant because of the faithfulness of God. Cone develops the meaning of this with "the biblical concept of the righteousness of God."[6] That is something the Israelites came to know in the exodus event. And for Cone the content of righteousness is justice. That is what God does in human history because justice is God's essential nature. "Divine righteousness means that God will be faithful to his promise, that his purposes for Israel will not be thwarted."[7] God's work in history is putting right what humankind has made wrong, even when at the moment it may not appear to be happening.

Cone solidifies his position with the claim that God is black. Black and white, of course, are ontological symbols for states of being – the state of being oppressed or being the oppressor. In calling God black, Black Theology is making clear where in the world God is and what is God doing. And this enables Cone to affirm the transition from then to now, from the exodus to the slave ships. What God did in Egypt God is now doing in America. The "epoch-making event" does not nullify the saving, liberating work. Cone does not want to yield either on goodness or power of God. He does not deny that "historical events seemed to contradict their faith in God as Liberator of the oppressed."[8] Clearly there are times when this God does not intervene. Blacks continue to be humiliated; oppression persists. But this does not lead Cone away from the God of Righteousness. Black Theology continues to affirm that God is where liberation is happening. The freedom movement out of Egypt and out of American racism is the authentic work of God. In short, Black Theology continues to tell the story of Israel's God and of the poor and oppressed of our time as if they were one. And the church is the agent of that message.

Cone rejects the reality of suffering as just punishment or even as an interruption on the road to another life. He does affirm that suffering can be redemptive. Those who are chosen are elected for service, not privilege. They are called into the mission of God in human history which is to bring about justice; their agenda is "to suffer with God in the divine realization of justice in the world."[9] Election and suffering are correlated because we have a "suffering God." And what makes the suffering on behalf of others redemptive is that God is present in the suffering. That means the evil experienced will not prevail. The power of the oppressor to humiliate and hurt will be taken away. The black God has made their cause God's own and "the oppressed are called to fight against suffering by becoming God's suffering servants in the world."[10] Their fight for freedom now is made credible by the history of God's faithfulness to God's promises. It is precisely in slavery and its aftermath to this day that there is a saving presence. The freedom movement is the exodus all over again. The experience of the black people draws them inexorably into the exodus event as their own. Slavery is an epoch making event which threatens the faith but for Cone does not prevail against it.

Cone does not shrink from the task of conveying the density and persistence of oppression. From the slave ships to the lynch mobs, from selling off family members like cattle, to segregated schools inadequately funded, from the devastation of African culture, to the turning of a people's religion against them, the black reality has been relentless oppression, humiliation and depersonalization. And it continues in ever-new forms to this day. But, Cone does make a move in relation to others who suffer unjustly when he invokes black and white as symbols for the states of being oppressed or being the oppressor. This is an inclusive move. "The focus on blackness does not mean that *only* blacks suffer as victims in a racist society, but that blackness is an ontological symbol and a visible symbol which best describes oppression in America." He goes on to embrace under the image of blackness "the extermination of Amerindians, the persecution of Jews, the oppression of Mexican-Americans, ... Black stands for all victims of oppression who realize that the survival of their humanity is bound up with liberation from whiteness."[11]

Blacks have experienced "244 years of slavery" that are still with us.[12] The Civil War may have formally ended slavery but the reality was that of relentless efforts "to keep black people a dependent and disciplined labor force."[13] The phenomenon of sharecropping "locked them into a system in which they were deep in debt" which prevented them from exiting their position.[14] Over the years stereotyping has resulted in "the absolute denial of the capacity for critical intelligence."[15] The aftermath of "244 years of slavery and 80-odd years of Jim Crowism" has impeded the development of independent and viable institutions with which to represent their interests.[16]

Black Theology and Resistance

There is no doubt in the mind of James Cone that there is a Black Theology. And it is white theology which is threatened by the black experience. He certainly intends that this "state religion" is radically exposed to the history that begins on the slave ships.

The theological project of which Cone is the progenitor is relentlessly situational. Black Theology does not begin in councils and creeds, in libraries and seminary offices, in established churches and their hierarchies. In the "Preface to the 1986 Edition" of *A Black Theology of Liberation*, Cone writes, "theology is not universal language about God... Theology is *contextual* language – that is, defined by the human situation that gives birth to it."[17] And for that, the white theological establishment cannot set the ground rules. Black Theology begins in the silenced of the earth and their struggle for justice. In a white world the black experience is one "where babies are tortured, women are raped, and men are shot." It is a system of slavery in which whites "attempt to define blacks as non-persons."[18] It is the "death dealing political, economic, and social structures of society."[19] It is being "bought and sold as a chattel." It is as a people to be "completely stripped of their African heritage".[20]

And it all "begins in 1619 when twenty black Africans were sold as indentured servants at Jamestown, Virginia..."[21] "Physical slavery was cruel. It meant working fifteen to twenty hours per day and being beaten unmercifully if one displayed the slightest fatigue. The auction block became a symbol of 'brokenness' because no family ties were recognized. Husbands were separated from wives and children from parents... their owners could dispose of them as they saw fit."[22] Theology begins in "flesh and blood" history, not universals or abstractions. Extinction was a prospect but exploitation was the norm in slavery and for Cone "progress" is more evident in refinements than in transformation of the social order.

The threat of Black Theology clusters around the religion of the status quo rather than the faith grounded in Scripture. Fundamentally, white theology is ideology. By ideology Cone means "deformed thought, ... a certain idea or ideas are nothing but the function of the subjective interests of a few.[23] The wishes, needs or desires of a person or community create distorted versions of reality. "Indeed, the economic and social interest" of a few" serve as a grid which prevents truth from being represented, or at least aspects of it.[24] White theology is really ideology. Rather than explicate the liberating message of tradition, it sanctions the present order and the privileges it insures. As such it is a "servant of the state" and undergirds racist and oppressive structures. Therefore, "it is not Christian theology at all."[25] Its fatal flaw is that it is "dispassionate analysis of 'the tradition' unrelated to the sufferings of the oppressed."[26] Far from calling in question the institutions and structures of the society, it gives them divine sanction. The prophetic tradition is aborted in favor of the values and interests of the privileged. A more intense threat of black experience/theology to white theology forms around the claim of "white distortion of God" and references to a "blood thirsty white idol." Cone goes on to assert that "God has nothing to do with the God worshipped in white churches whose primary purpose is to sanctify the racism of white and daub the wounds of blacks."[27]

When one considers the role of Scripture in Cone's theology, the first issue is, "Who does the reading?" It is this question that gives rise to a defense against the charge that Cone's theology is also an ideology. The content/context factor in interpretation discussed in Chapter three is crucial here. The white reading of Scripture called upon slaves to be obedient to their masters. The slaves reading of the text "denuded" of the oppressive rendering that "enabled slaves to affirm a view of God that differed radically from that of slave masters."[28] The Scriptures did not teach them to be better slaves but liberated ones. Cone argues that their situation enabled them to understand the exodus story as their own. The exodus account is of a God who neither sleeps nor slumbers but takes a stand with the slaves against the slave masters. Scripture for the slaves and for the black community is not opaque but transparent. There is an "interplay of social context with Scripture"; the "concreteness of everyday life" corresponds with the biblical narrative.[29] "Then-and-there" become "here-and-now." For James Cone "Christian theology begins and ends with the biblical story of God's liberation of the weak."[30]

Rituals and Resistance

As we have noted before, a ritual is a "repeatable form."[31] And it is not something we can really avoid. It can, of course, become meaningless and empty but that is only to acknowledge that some rituals emerge and may pass away, or at least become dysfunctional. However, free of one, others prevail. Rituals are something we cannot avoid doing. We never outgrow them. While they are not inevitably religious, there is no religion without them. The civil rights movement is a consummate example. While a political statement in its own right, Martin Luther King undergirded it with religious symbols and rituals.

But more has been said than that it is a "repeatable form." Driver writes that "they are born out of necessity, ... and the people who best know that life is difficult are the ones most likely to cleave to ritual and make it work for them."[32] One might say that through ritual we negotiate the realities of our lives – the times of chaos, complexity, danger, joy, and celebration. Through them we learn, transmit, and rehearse what culture has yielded through the generations. As noted before, "To ritualize is to make (or utilize) a pathway through what would otherwise be uncharted territory."[33] As it is repeated it may become more like a "shelter" and less like a "pathway."[34] For the most part it is something we inherit, though we can indeed invent new forms. Rituals not only "repeat the known but also extend the frontier."[35] As such, rituals can be thought of as coping mechanisms, ones that defy the boundaries set by agents of empire.

Ritual is essential to the divine–human interaction. It is the means by which we invoke, address, or effect an "unseen power." Ritual connects the immediate realities of our lives with something believed to be beyond them. The sacred is perceived to be here in religious rituals and here in a way which enables coping or negotiating our way through what we are facing. Again, Driver writes, "A ritual is an efficacious performance that invokes the presence and action of powers which, without ritual, would not be present or active at that time and place, …."[36] They put us in touch with what we can trust; and they both affirm order and promise transformation.

James Cone may not employ the formal language of liturgy and ritual but it is integral to his Black Theology. If we remember that ritual is a "repeatable form" and that it is a "pathway" and a "shelter" through which to negotiate the realities at hand, then the spirituals in particular and worship in general qualify and provide grounds for comparison.

For James Cone, Black Theology has its roots in the A.M.E. Church which shaped his Christian identity. "Every Sunday and sometimes on weeknights I encountered Jesus through rousing sermons, fervent prayers, spirited gospel songs, and the passionate testimonies of the people."[37] It was the expressions of faith in the Macedonian Church that created an armor which resisted the white definition of blacks as inferior. When surrounded by the degradation at the hands of the white inhabitants, Cone and his fellow worshippers were assured there was an ultimate justice which would prevail. With the clapping and shouting, dancing and stamping, the Spirit was in their midst empowering them to "keep on keeping on" and sustain their sense of being defined by a liberating God. The troubles of their daily lives could be negotiated because there One who was "a very present help in times of trouble."[38] All the onslaught of racism could not threaten the faith that they were God's children. Indeed, "they preached sermons about loving God and thy neighbor as if the violence that whites committed against blacks did not invalidate their Christian identity."[39] And when some critics of his first two books suggested his theology was not adequately grounded in the black experience, Cone wrote an autobiographical introduction to his most sophisticated book. And upfront he affirmed the black church experience as the matrix of his faith and the centerpiece of his theology. "Through prayer, song, and sermon, God made frequent visits to the black community in Bearden and reassured the people of his concern for their well-being and his will to bring them safely home."[40] His critics did not understand that his theology all along emerged from the environment of ritual and secured its credibility there. The racism in Bearden, finding its most acute expression in a lynch mob's quest for his Father, not only did not threaten their faith but deepened its grip upon them. Ritual yielded a saving presence.

No one who has visited a black church could confuse its worship with that of a white church, at least not a mainstream church. And a primary reason for that is that slavery was the cradle of black worship. It "has been wrought out of the experience of slavery and lynching... Black worship was born on slave ships and nurtured in cotton fields...."[41] Authentic worship is connected to the lived reality of people and cannot be understood apart from it. The confidence that "God would make a way out of no way" was not grounded in rationality, scientific evidence, or dogma but in the worship which yielded a God whose saving purpose will not be thwarted.

To understand this in all its richness we need to focus on the spirituals in particular. Black survival in slavery and its aftermath is integrally related to "the power of the song." It is appropriate to give attention to black music as music and Cone does that. But it is more appropriate to investigate it theologically. It is the language of the Spirit which kept alive community and self-determination in the midst of relentless attempts to destroy both. Cone maintains that "there is a complex world of *thought* underlying the slave songs"[42] and that world was one of resistance in the power of the Divine Presence. The spirituals were not vehicles for accommodation to the slave-master's brutality or for postponed fulfillment in another world. Rather, they brought into existence the realization that then-and-there is here-and-now. The righteous will prevail in history and the unrighteous will be punished. The spirituals are freedom songs here-and-now; "de God dat lived in Moses time is jus de same today."[43] Spirituals not only sprung out of the environment of slavery but functioned there as assurance a Divine Presence would liberate them. The spirituals are "historical songs that speak about the rupture of black lives ... and what they did to hold themselves together and fight back ... Through songs, they built new structures for existence in an alien land."[44] And this was only possible because God was involved in their history and would deliver them from their plight as God had the Israelites in the exodus. Slavery is a contradiction of the divine will and as such cannot persist. Freedom is not about the future singularly but about the present. And the resurrection of Jesus meant more than a heavenly destiny. Jesus is alive and in their midst as a "divine guarantee that their lives are in the hands of him who conquered death."[45]

Cone acknowledges that heaven is a central image in the spirituals. And inevitably it brings to mind a future not of this world. But he argues that the notion of heaven in the spirituals had earthly implications. Sometimes it even had an earthly destination. The referent was Canada, up north, or Africa. Often, more realistically, "the idea of heaven provided ways for black people to affirm their humanity... It enabled them to say yes to their right to be free..."[46]

God is the assurance of their "somebodiness" and therefore works in them resistance to their nonperson environment. Defined by the liberating God, rather than the dehumanizing white master, the hope generated by the spirituals "enabled black slaves to risk their lives for earthly freedom because they knew they had a home 'over yonder'."[47]

Black worship and the spirituals are fashioned in historical oppression and claim the faith that what God has done before, God is doing now. They are the practice of hope and the assurance resistance is not in vain.

Earlier we noted James Cone's determination to destroy white theology. The articles of faith are under the jurisdiction of the oppressor and are used as weapons to humiliate and inflict suffering. The slave-masters artfully used the symbols of faith to sanction the prevailing order and to preempt resistance. The one who controls the symbols controls reality and defines the place of others in it. On the negative side, then, securing the symbols means wrestling them away from the oppressor. At another level, it means enabling them to work for the oppressed on the assumption that is a return to their original meaning. That is Cone's most persistent task in reading the Scriptures from his location.

While the options are many for development, the symbol that needs attention is that of reconciliation. It is a classic example of "the master's tools." The tone of Cone's early writings in particular might seem to make reconciliation an unlikely choice. But it is the very passion of that rhetoric that makes it a necessary one. Symbols are integrally related to the story we tell ourselves, and religious symbols authenticate it. In the white narrative, truth-telling ought to accord with reconciliation. Doesn't God love everyone the same, and isn't God's will that we live together in peace and goodwill? To forgive and forget is the white content to reconciliation. But, Cone argues, "We must refuse to let whites define the terms of reconciliation."[48] That bottoms out in "feel good" theology.

Cone is quite clear that Paul's claim that Christ is "our peace, who has made us... one, and has broken down the dividing wall of hostility" does not mean "that the hostility between black and whites has been brought to an end." It is true for Cone that in the Bible reconciliation is an act of God but it is something related to the wrath of God which preempts sentimental version of the love of God. Wrath is a function of righteousness which means God is faithful to God's reality. And "Righteousness is that side of God's love which expresses itself through black liberation."[49] What comes of it is a destruction of whiteness (oppression) and the creation of blackness (freedom). Reconciliation is made possible by Divine liberation 'from Economic, social, political bondage."[50] So the content of reconciliation is what God is doing to free the oppressed and defeat the oppressors. In short, no liberation, no reconciliation; no justice, no peace; no freedom, no fellowship. Therefore, "To be reconciled is to be set free; ...(and). It means participation in God's revolutionizing activity in the world, changing the political, economic, and social structure so that the distinction between rich and poor, oppressed and oppressors, are no longer a reality."[51] Reconciliation begins in rebellion, God instigated, and ends when there are no more masters. And no more empire! The faith, nurtured by the church and articulated theologically, has prevailed.

EPILOGUE

CHAPTER NINE

Christians are confident nothing in this world is eternal, permanent, or inevitable; yet empire creates the impression it is an exception, the only one! And the church often complies. Empire rules "...not only, and not even primarily, by punitive force, but rather through the propagation of an ideology that persuades most people to believe that there is no point to resist because destiny has made things the way they are."[1] Empire may be unique in its capacity to penetrate all dimensions of our social, economic and political life without provoking doubts about its legitimacy and power. Its narrative and stories create and reflect reality; that is the "public transcript" and it persists.

The church is a community with a "hidden transcript" which threatens the reign of Caesar. It subverts the empire. Even the existence of its Scripture is a direct challenge. Thatcher ends his book with the words: "The church is Rome in reverse."[2] It is anointed and driven by "counter-memories"[3] which may not dispute the facts of history but have a contrasting take on what is happening through them. Because it lives from "the God of endings," it positions itself in persistent opposition. That the church understands itself as "Rome in reverse" does not mean it grooves on negation like an "acid reflex." It is more simply, oppositional. It lives in a counter-memory which at its core reads history differently. The church is not "the loyal opposition;" loyalty is fixed on the God of the exodus and the resurrection. Thus, the "hidden transcript" contradicts and upends the "public transcript" and falsifies it. The claims of Caesar are canceled. As was argued earlier, the titles attached to Caesar and his regime are usurped and designates the identity of Jesus. Even the arrogance of Caesar cannot absorb that offense. It is hardly benign symbol lending. Titular castration is more than outrageous; it is grounds for crucifixion. And it came to that.

We have acknowledged that the temptation of the church is to package itself and its message in terms that not only are acceptable to empire but reflect its values. At times, it yields. Empire seeps into its consciousness and distorts its message and mission. In the context of a market society, for example, the church may take on the reality and methods of the prevailing order. The church of Christ can become subverted by a "pervasive and hegemonic" economic system. "Many churches have become like firms competing for market shares (converts). So churches develop a product (i.e. the message) that appeals to the taste of consumers in general, or they specialize for a specific segment of the consumer market."[4] The stamp of the economic empire is defining and indelible. The sacred and the secular merge in a community which has forfeited its prophetic distance.

The Empire State Building may not be a national Vatican, but it comes close. It functions as a sacred symbol in the midst of the collusion of financial interests. What may not be well-known is that two of its floors are occupied by an institution which blends nationalism with elements of the religious right. King's College moved there in 1999 where it proudly, even arrogantly, distinguishes itself from secular institutions of higher education. The Chancellor of the College writes in the handbook for students concerning other colleges, "almost all their professors' traffic in spent ideas that do not work – bad ideas that have had myriad of disastrous consequences in our generation. They are wrong about God, human nature, wealth, power, marriage, poverty, family, sex, America, liberty, peace and many other decisive issues." The institutional goal is to create "ambassadors of Jesus Christ to lead and serve the world."[5] The students live in dormitories named for persons like a Ronald Reagan and Margaret Thatcher. The Empire State Building is situated in the vicinity of others whose vulnerability was established on 9/11/01. In the heart of the NYC beast Jesus is wrapped in red, white, and blue and is served by an advanced guard in whom piety, consumer capitalism, and salvation are blended. Echoes of empire and consumptive Christianity are merged to save the world, one city at a time. Once again, Rome has become sacred in our time. It is incumbent upon the church to differentiate itself from empire. That clarification is a precondition of recognizing the seepage of empire into the life of the church.

The Church as Rome in Reverse

The first distinction is that empire has no bad memories. It has no sense of having been or contemplating being dead wrong. Empire lives with the confidence it is always "on the mark" and any ambiguity about its message or mission is unlikely and inadmissible. Any failure to prevail is not a function of a deficit in empire's agenda or commitment. The church, by contrast, can be profoundly aware of the times in which it has not been true to its heritage. Rather than Rome in reverse it has often been congenial with what should be its adversaries. In particular, there are two strikingly bad memories: the realities of racism and the horrors of the Holocaust. At its best the church has the courage and the integrity to embrace its history without being in denial about is worst moments. Denial is a permanent state for empire.

Since we have given some attention to race, the Holocaust deserves to be acknowledged and the failures of the church in the face of it. While this default is not total, it is still a devastating memory when cast against its commitment to love and justice. While the exceptions are remarkable and bold, the silence of the church at large is a haunting reality. Michael Berenbaum holds up the fact that "new thresholds of inhumanity" were reached in the Holocaust with unprecedented goals and unparalled methods.[6] Extermination of Jews became even more important at times than winning the war. The right of Jews to exist was canceled at every conceivable point. While a pregnancy might normally be the occasion for joy, in Auschwitz it was a death sentence for both the mother and unborn child. It made no difference that the pregnancy was often the result of a forced liaison with a German guard. Children who had no capacity for work as well as those whose energies were exhausted in work were void of moral consideration. The expected relief and refreshment of a shower, even when mercilessly crowded, was an occasion for hope until the gas rather than water gushed from the shower heads. The elevation of a few prisoners with privileges and authority to subjugate the many was common place and subverted bonds of respect and affection. No wonder Emil Fackenheim argues, "Never, within or without Jewish history, have men anywhere had such dreadful such horrifying, reason for turning their backs on the God of history."[7] It is not surprising that many came to believe that the God of the exodus was either in eclipse or engaged in cruel disregard of a chosen people.

The point of recalling the default on race and the Holocaust is not to obsess on the past but to embrace it as a haunting memory yet one that calls forth the response, "never again" in our time. Empire has no tolerance for failures and no recognition of it when it happens. It is in perpetual denial of its warped past. The Grace of God enables the church to face its moral lapses and be empowered by them. The church can embrace the loving and the horrific and be enabled by both as impetuses to engage in its mission: to put love and justice together in history. Race and the Holocaust are reminders of events perpetrated by empire – and the church when it was in collusion – which are embraced by the faith community in repentance and empowerment. The church is not afraid to begin in its past failures in order not to repeat them. The church reverses Rome by courageous embrace of a past marked by violating its heritage. Certitude and absolutizing are alien to its nature.

The consideration in chapter two about power and weakness is fair ground for the second distinction between empire and church. The texture of empire is power; it is fundamental to its reality. Empire embodies power, it exercises power, and it overpowers when challenged. As a superpower on the global scene, its every move is to insure against opposition; it cannot tolerate competition. Empire's need and determination to prevail is without equal and without compromise. Its reach is global and its resolve is relentless. Nothing escapes its control and everything is within its legitimate jurisdiction. Empire takes power to the nth degree and glories in its unqualified mastery of events.

By contrast, the texture of the church is weakness. It exercises its weakness in all affairs and ironically prevails by weakness. Its manner of defense is defenselessness. The church has no aspiration to defeat empire on some battlefield; it is content to be empire in reverse on its own turf. Inversion is endemic to its reality. John D. Caputo invites the Christian community "to stop thinking about God as a massive ontological power line that provides power to the world, instead of thinking of something that short-circuits such power and provides a provocation of the world that is otherwise than power."[8] Caputo goes on to say about the Kingdom of God in Jesus teaching, "the weak forces play themselves out in paradoxical effects that confound the powers that be, displaying the unsettling shock delivered in the reigning order by the name of God."[9] Christ is not imperial and nothing imperial seeps into his preaching, parables, and interventions.

A church that is transparent to that Kingdom and its God is threatening precisely because it is "other" to the empire. Its texture is characterized "by madness of forgiveness, generosity, mercy and hospitality."[10] This is not to suggest that the message of the Kingdom is unidirectional and can only be evident as pacifism. Unconditional love and commitment to justice can take multiple forms but will always be marked by weakness. The church is the community of the improbable standing up to empire which assumes the reality of the probable. In the measure it is an extension of the incarnation in our time, it is not heroic or even impressive. Its hero is not a superhero or even a heroic one in any sense. "What is most inviting about Jesus is that he is defeated, executed, and abandoned, that he is a man whose symbol is an instrument of public execution, and whose message is radical peace."[11] When a disciple attempts to defend him with a sword, he proclaims that things are not done that way in God's Kingdom. Even as his disciples desert him, he forgives those who would crucify him. He expresses abandonment by God much as some victims of the Holocaust did. There is no quick fix on Friday. On the cross he "is not an icon of power but of powerlessness."[12] No exercise of force was evident; everything was on hold until Easter morning. The weakness of God hesitated on Friday but prevailed on Sunday as the women found the tomb empty of everything but powerlessness.

The church reverses empire in that it lives from a failed life, announces forgiveness for the unforgiveable, offers mercy to those who need it whether or not they deserve it, and embraces the unembraceable with food, shelter, acceptance, and a measure of hope for a new future. In a sense, the church has no fear of being seen as pathetic or without "the right stuff!" The apostle Paul refers to Christians as "fools for Christ;" and he also offers the weakness of God as the power that can transform the world by refusing to emulate the world when it steps into and lives history. Unlike the empire, the church is the community through which the weakness of God translates into food for the hungry, shelter for the homeless, freedom for the captives, and hope for the destitute. In this sense, it is Rome in reverse. Rome's energies are exhausted in self-preservation. The church is energized and empowered by what is beyond. Empire thinks of food and shelter as commodities; God sees them as necessities for the hungry and homeless.

Nowhere is "Rome in reverse" more evident than in relation to the cross. As has been argued, the cross is the fullest expression of empire; it has jurisdiction over life and death. At every point the cross is a bold statement of who controls reality and its success in doing so. In a sense, it is not who is crucified that matters as much as who has the power to do it. While violent and degrading, it is "a scripted index of Roman imperial power."[13] It is the ultimate evidence of total control in history. Symbolically it is an unambiguous statement of whose world this is.

The church puts the cross on the altar; it defines the cross as its ultimate symbol of resistance and triumph. While the reign of Caesar was presumed to be established on Good Friday, Caesar ultimately is the victim not the victor. For the church the cross represents whose world this really is. Caesar may think he is God, but there is a transcendent One within the event. There is a foreshadowing of this in the trial of Jesus before Pilate. This was an event in which "Herod and Pilate became friends" (Luke 23:12). They were one in fixating on Jesus' guilt: was he or wasn't he? Pilate was attempting to sustain his own innocence by listening for the voice of the crowd. Pilate had "wondered" that Jesus did nothing to defend himself. He was silent, powerless! (Mark 15:5). Pilate said to Jesus, "You will not speak to me? Do you not know that I have power to release you, and power to crucify you?" Jesus answered him, "You would have no power over me unless it had been given you from above; therefore he who delivered me to you has the greater sin" (John 19:10-11). Jesus turns the issue of guilt into one of authority. God is implicated in the event. Caesar is only a vessel.

One reason the cross is the central symbol for the church is the realization that God grasps history at its most horrific points. God enters when the Israelites are victims of the Egyptians and when Jesus is set up for crucifixion. God enters at the point of powerlessness and leads beyond it. No wonder the poor and oppressed have a "hermeneutical privilege;" they know where God is because they know where God has been. Christians have often cheapened the injunction of Jesus to "take up your cross and follow me." The cross is not some inconvenience or set back. It is where God has penetrated history and leads it on toward a new future. God is where the poor, powerless, and oppressed cry out for freedom. The cross is where the power of empire meets the powerlessness of Jesus and announces that the freedom struggle has begun and will prevail. The last words of Jesus on the cross are, "It is finished." To the Romans, and the empire, that meant they won. Thatcher contends, "his mission and the Scripture are 'completed' when he dies (John 19:28-30). Christ 'cast out the ruler of this world' (12:31) at the very moment when he seemed to fall to imperial power. Caesar was the true victim at Calvary."[14] The church is not called to flee to Easter until it has grasped the movement of God in crucifixion. For Martin Luther King the cross is the freedom struggle and "taking up your cross (means) to live a life dedicated to love and justice in personal and political life."[15]

For the church, the cross is empowering – not in the sense of overpowering – but of enabling to "keep on keeping on." Caesar's power was broken on the cross. Ironically, the victor becomes victim and the victim becomes victor. The church can live "in the knowledge Caesar has been conquered in the revelation through Jesus."[16] The church always lives in empire's shadow, yet its mission is to be at one with where God engages history. While empire is always on the alert for events which might challenge its control, the church stealthfully is on the alert for the irruptions in history which the cross names as the work of God for justice. The recognition of where God is, and whom God is with, is an empowering summons to be the church.

The church is "Rome in reverse" when it takes the cross off the altar and from around the neck of followers and embraces it as a cipher of where God is breaking in and breaking up. There covenants are formed as the faith community embraces, in solidarity with God and the victims, the cause of love and its public form as justice. The bonding of the church with God enables the church to be true to its mission in history. It is significant that the crucifixion of Jesus took place during the celebration of the Passover in which the Israelites celebrate deliverance from empire. In the economy of God, the Passover defined the deeper meaning of the crucifixion. It sets the church to the task of being "Rome in reverse." And this rebellion looks strangely like a community living the resurrection of Jesus. There a transcending power enables the faith community to be the cross of Jesus in the world. Confident that Easter morning always follows, the Grace of God lifts the faith community off its fears and empowers it to embrace its mission.

In the time of empire the church is the community that lives in the crucifixion narrative with Easter morning on the horizon.

Strategies for Subverting Empire

That the church is called by the biblical witness to a posture of resistance in the power of its resources results in a positive agenda. At their best, negatives have affirmations embedded in them. And action results from reflection or should. In *The Rebel*, Albert Camus wrote ("Rebellion's") "most profound logic is not the logic of destruction; it is the logic of creation."[17] New orders arise from discerning the injustices of old ones. Resistance in its most authentic form is revelatory. Dissent provides the occasion for disclosure. Discerning critiques expose inordinate possibilities and who creates them. The church as "Rome in reverse" yields an alternative scripting of reality which arises out of the demise of the old. Resistance enhances resources; indeed, it surfaces them. To rebel is not simply to expose the contours of the present order; it is to enable something radically new to emerge. Indeed, Mark Lewis Taylor has argued that rebellion is revelatory in "imitating insights and as unveiling a fullness of meaning."[18] The Civil Rights movement beginning in the 1960's was an act of rebellion against and resistance to oppression of the African American community. But in the mind of Martin Luther King it was a reflection of the exodus from Egypt. Resistance opens history to its possibilities.

The point of the church in the form of resistance to empire is not a reckless violation which leaves the global community in a state of dysfunctional chaos. The point of critiquing the dynamic of global capitalism, for example, is not to leave the economy in shambles; as we noted, it is to reshape the system so that "access to livelihood" is assured. The goal is to make the system work for all. Neither the rich nor the poor would be served by a destruction of the economic order. Marxism may have some discerning insights but it is not a viable programming of the global order. The market cannot be so cavalierly displaced. It would wreak havoc. Contrary to some popular myths, liberation theology is not Marxist even as it may affirm some of the insights of that ideology. In the last chapter James Cone fashioned theological exercises around radical social change. While liberation theology and Marxism may identity some of the same problems, the solutions are grounded in praxis not ideology.

Theologians are not usually addicted to identifying practical agendas! Theological reflection is more rewarding. But it cannot be an end in itself if it is to be transformative. The Salvadorian priest/ theologian, Ignacio Ellacuria, raised the voice of the oppressed and focused on the injustices of his society. But he also wrote, "Action without contemplation is empty and destructive, while contemplation without action is paralyzing and concealing."[19] Or, in other words, love and justice are inseparable for the theologian and the faith community. Faith without consequences is as disastrous as consequences without faith. The Christian tradition calls for both reflection and action. The one flows from the other and is a fulfillment of it as well.

If the church is to engage in the dialectic of reflection and action, it needs to be clear about its own identity. It is important for the faith community to assess its authenticity, to be clear about whose it is and what it has to say, and to examine its ecclesial practices. In a sense, it needs to take its pulse before being programmatic. Consideration of the role of Scripture and the nature of worship are essential. Most churches give some attention to the Bible; it receives some attention from the preacher on Sunday mornings. But neither is the same as setting the study of Scripture as the center piece of the churches life; it is not the same as making it the first order of business. The community needs to put in place conscientious study in the manner we explored in chapter three. This includes attending to the context within which the message emerged and considering what is at play in a contemporary hearing. This is all simply to argue that the Bible needs to move from being one of the options to the controlling activity of the faith community. That is the only way to become clear about the churches identity and message.

Part of what follows from this is critical reflection on the worship of the church. There is a history of being casual about the way the faith comes forward on Sunday mornings. No wonder there is "ritual boredom" as Tom Driver says. The temptation is to think because one has sung a few hymns, listened to the choir and Scripture lesson and sermon, and closed one's eyes for prayer, that we have "done it for this week." It would be somewhat unusual for a faith community to ask, how should we worship in the face of empire? Has empire seeped into the setting and substance of worship? Does our worship equip us for the action called for by the Gospel? In chapter five we considered the sacraments and ways in which they could be framed and fashioned so this served a political agenda, one that is liberating from empire. Empire calls for worship; the task of the church is to worship in ways which draft its resources for resistance. Along with attention to Scripture, it needs to be a consuming priority.

It is incumbent upon us now to ground our analysis of the church in a time of empire in some specific strategic agendas. Walter Brueggemann has written that "human transformation ... does not happen through didacticism or through excessive certitude, but through the playful entertainment of another scripting of reality ." [20] How do the resources available for resistance take form in the church in its struggle with the reality of empire? What might the scripting look like? What are the practical consequences or forms of being "Rome in reverse"? Specifically, how might the church "short circuit" – without disabling - the systems of the world and creating chaos?

It is important first to return to the discussion of *ekklesia* and the ways it discloses the meaning of church. The word leads Elisabeth

Schüssler Fiorenza to note that "this very self-description of the early church community was a radical democratic one."[21] It is an open and welcoming setting where privilege has been pre-empted. Fiorenza and others feminists modify the term with "women," not only to offset the history of male domination, but to surface the reality of a "democratic ethos." Privilege in power and discourse is pre-empted. The voices of all are heard and honored. In a sense, it is an open society for dialogue and decision-making. As a consortium of equals, diversity is welcomed and ultimate resolution is anticipated. One need not be timid and one dare not claim unambiguous certitude. Fiorenza is exposing the authentic organization and texture of a "democratic congress."

In this context the church has traditionally made pronouncements about issues in the world. The Catholic Church in particular has a long history of social teaching. Other Christian communities speak to the world and its institutions as well. But, there is an alternative to pronouncements alone. The church, if formed as an authentic *ekklesia*, can invite the world/society with its divergent agendas into its midst. Thus, it can move beyond a consideration among its members to offering itself as a venue in which contesting parties are invited in to participate in a democratic dialogue. The issues generated by America as an empire, and the forms it takes in society, can be explored in what was thought to be only sacred space. Think, for example, of the tortured political discourses over balanced budgets vs. social programs. The ethos of empire is so penetrated by power that judicious discourse is not an outcome. Someone has to win – and it tends to be those who always have. Or, consider issues generated by a capitalistic economy. Its markets work for those who have the wealth to prime it. Others have no voice. The church could be a setting where empire is de-sacralized and opened up for rational discourse among respected parties. Or, consider the issues surrounding the prison system and the death penalty. Empire thinks they make us more secure. The church could be a setting where justice and humane institution could be debated.

Or consider the issue of immigration, the protection of jobs and the recognition of legitimate human needs. Those deserve judicious dialogue. Politians wrangle over each other's motives, consistency, and integrity. Posturing is relentless. And the issues and those who suffer from it are seldom openly addressed. Secular discourse calls for another space; potentially, the church has it.

If the church really can sustain a "democratic ethos" of mutual respect it could become an arena in which the tentacles of empire are exposed and excised and issues are judiciously addressed. American society needs a setting in which honest discourse can prevail and resolution can emerge. The objection might emerge that this could destroy the church and provoke destructive divisions. But that is a risk the church can take if it is to be faithful to its own values and the faith tradition that permeates it. Because of who God has been in Christ, the church can engage in a playful scripting which enables it to share its "democratic ethos" with a society that has forfeited that ethos. The church is a community that prevails by the grace of God and not the might of men/women. Unlike empire, self-preservation is not an agenda.

A second aspect of the relationship of the church to empire is an extension of its reality as *ekklesia*. The early church was surrounded by, and even invaded by, "kyriarchal models of household and state in antiquity which were governed by the lord/master/father head of the house" relationships .[22] Kyriarchy is a social ordering which is "top down" and marked by domination and subordination. Dualisms, binary constructions, and hierarchies establish the fabric of individual interactions and social institutions. Everything is about privilege and power. The early church had to struggle against kyriarchal arrangements in its common life. The significant point of Fiorenza's argument is that *ekklesia* drives out kyriarchy; at every point it names it, subverts it, and exorcises it. Privilege and power relationships are not in its DNA.

This suggests a strategy for the church in its struggle with empire. As has been argued in relation to power, relations of domination and subordination are the handiwork of empire. It depends on kyriarchal relationships and institutions to achieve its control of reality. When the church has been true to its origin it has achieved an equalitarian state. Galatians makes it clear: "there is neither Jew nor Greek, there is neither slave nor free, there is neither male nor female; for you are all one in Christ Jesus" (3:28). Diversity and unity do not preempt each other in a community arising from the Christ event. As Brigitte Kahl notes, the church is "radically detached from the bloodline of empire."[23] That provides a unique opportunity for prophetic action. One could render the Galatians text in contemporary terms: there is neither black nor white, gay nor straight, rich nor poor, first world nor third world, male nor female but all are one in Christ Jesus. In the measure the church is the body of Christ, it is an egalitarian community, equals with differences that do not differentiate in divisive ways.

The church, then, as ekklesia is a model of community in which the humanity of all is affirmed and human flourishing is a reality. It would be an illusion to claim that the church is always in that mode. But it is the community which knows what it is meant to be. And, therefore, it has the responsibility to "call out" the kyriarchal nature of society and its institutions. This is not to retreat into exceptionalism; the church is not empowered to name the world and then control those in it. The church is a "light unto the world" in the sense that its rays expose and subvert the forms of subordination and domination in the world order. Of course, the world is not "in Christ"! But the church knows and deciphers the violations of justice and equality and cannot refrain from "naming the beasts" in the social order.

Because of the unity in Christ the church is obligated to "call out" violations of the integrity of same-sex relationships, to "call out" the ways in which economic policy privileges the powerful, to "call out" racial profiling, to "call out" discriminatory institutions and laws which punish those who are "other," to "call out" government laws and policies which inhibit meeting the basic needs of people, to "call out" whatever in our society creates homelessness. This is not to engender self-righteousness in the faith community but to enable the weakness of God to be made evident in the structures of society. Resistance to empire can take the form of the church using its resources to model for the world a "democratic ethos" and subvert the values, institution, and system which sustain domination and subordination. That would be evidence of a playful scripting of reality.

Third, the claiming of resources for the initiative of resistance has its origin in the Christ event. Jürgen Moltmann provides a framework for a strategy. "Christ's resurrection begins in the world of the dead. He draws up Adam with his right hand and Eve with his left, and with them pulls humanity and the whole sighing creation out of the realm of the dead into the new transfigured world ... his raising from the dead is inclusive, open to the world, and embraces the universe ... (toward) the beginning of a new creation of all things."[24] In the profoundest sense, Moltmann is giving the secular realm a new dimension. While it is empire in nature, there is also what George Williamson calls "the breakthrough of God."[25] The world ruled and defined by empire is also the territory where a new beginning is emerging. It all begins "in the world of the dead" where the weakness of God surfaces and breaks open the cross and Easter morning once again. The secular is the setting where it is happening; it did once and it will again. Hence, the church is the community which sees evidence of new beginnings in old formations. Caesar's world has been visited by the God of Jesus Christ opening it up to a new future. Life comes from the arrangements and ordering of death.

That likely is a thick way of pointing to the cracks in empire's grasp and naming the new ordering of life. The church may resist the world but it has no right to reject or abandon it. It is loaded with secular resurrections. The struggle for justice and the arrival of a new order need not come in sacred gown or majestic places. It can come in a home for the homeless, in a food bank, or in a shelter for battered woman. The church is the community which has a sense of what love and justice look like – and Who is at work in it. Thus, one mission of the church is to aggressively make common cause with persons, institutions, and events which have the qualities of a "breakthrough of God." Because the church has images of what that looks like, it can name it for its own purposes and join it.

It is not the mission of the church in resistance to empire to engage in a lonely vigils or a solo protests. While the church does name the demons it is also responsible for joining the forces for justice. Reinhold Niebuhr used to tell his students that often there is more of the Gospel of love in Alcoholic Anonymous than in some churches. That is not so much because they "got it" as that they embraced it, often unknowingly. There is an overlap between AA and what God is doing to heal broken lives. The society may not be able to name God but that does not shut down God's activity. The "breakthrough of God" may come in the most unlikely places; the church can name them and suggest them without taking credit for them.

This is a way of saying the church may be the community that embodies the purposes of God but it does not have a "captured God," one confined to its premises. Human transformation and new scripting of reality can and do occur in God's world, not necessarily God's church. And the role of the church then becomes to make common cause with the eruption of justice in society wherever it occurs and in whatever form. It knows what a truly human community looks like and it can identify and struggle with its emergence. That's another playful scripting.

The church in the time of empire is called to live in Christ's resurrection and its mission is to join in the work of bringing a new creation out of the realm of death. That, however, does not translate into a mission to disable America as a nation. Quite the opposite, the church as a community of "honest patriots" is called to a new kind of patriotism – one that works toward the liberation of the nation from the clutches of empire and sets it free to embody its most authentic values.

END NOTES

Chapter One: THE CONTOURS OF EMPIRE

1 Donald W. Shriver, Jr., *Honest Patriots: Loving a Country Enough to Remember Its Misdeeds* (New York: Oxford University Press, 2008), 61.

2 Randall Robinson, *The Debt: What America Owes to Blacks* (New York: Penguin Books, 2000), 3.

3 Timothy H. Parsons, *The Rule of Empires: Those Who Built Them, Those Who Endured Them, and Why They Always Fail* (New York: Oxford University Press, 2010), 2.

4 Ibid., 4.

5 Michael Hardt and Antonio Negri, *Empire* (Cambridge, Massachusetts: Harvard University Press, 2001), xiv.

6 Madeline Albright, *The Mighty and the Almighty* (New York: Harper Collins Publishers, 2006), 30-32.

7 Andrew J. Bacevich, *The Limits of Power* (New York: Henry Holt and Company, 2008), 1.

8 John Winthrop, "A Model of Christian Charity" in Conrad Cherry, *God's New Israel* (Englewood Cliffs, New Jersey: Prentice-Hall, 1971), 42-43.

9 Godfrey Hodgson, *The Myth of American Exceptionalism* (New Haven: Yale University Press, 2009), 2.

10 Project For a New American Century, "Statement of Principles" June 3, 1997. Web: newamericancentury.org.

11 Ibid., i.

12 Michael Mandelbaum, *The Case for Goliath* (New York: Public

Affairs, 2005), xvi.

13 Ibid., 7.

14 Ibid., 4-5.

15 Ibid., 25.

16 The Project for the New American Century, Web page, "Iraq: Setting the Record Straight."

17 Ibid., ii.

18 Ibid., 13.

19 Jack Nelson-Pallmeyer, *Saving Christianity from Empire* (New York: Continuum International Publishing Group, 2005), 43.

20 Winthrop, "A Model of Christian Charity," 45.

21 George W. Bush, quoted in Nelson-Pallmeyer, 11.

22 Michael Doyle, quoted in Mandelbaum , The Case For Goliath, 4.

23 Mandelbaum, *The Case For Goliath*, 6.

24 Douglas Meeks, *God the Economist* (Minneapolis: Fortress Press, 1989), 65.

25 Reinhold Niebuhr, *The Structure of Nations and Empires* (New York: Charles Scribner's Sons, 1959), 203.

26 Ibid., 257.

Chapter Two: EMPIRE AND TRANSCENDENCE

1 Michael Mann, quoted in John Dominic Crossan, *God and Empire* (San Francisco: Harper Collins, 2007), 12.

2 John Dominic Crossan, *God and Empire* (San Francisco: Harper Collins, 2007), 13-14.

3 Catherine Keller, *God and Power* (Minneapolis: Fortress Press, 2005), 31.

4 George Ritzer, *The Globalization of Nothing* (Thousand Oaks, California: Pine George Press, 2003), 85.

5 Ibid., 86.

6 Ibid., 90.

7 Godfrey Hodgson, *The Myth of American Exceptionalism* (New Haven: Yale University Press, 2009), 159.

8 Ibid., 172.

9 Catherine Keller, "Omnipotence and Preemption" quoted in David Ray Griffin, et al, *The American Empire and the Commonwealth of God* (Louisville: Westminster John Knox, 2006), 124.

10 Joerg Rieger, "Christian Theology and Empires" in Kwok Pui-lan, *et al, Empire and the Christian Tradition* (Minneapolis: Fortress Press, 2007), 3.

11 Keller, *God and Power*, 31.

12 Paul King and David O. Woodyard, *Liberating Nature* (Cleveland: The Pilgrim Press, 1999), 85.

13 Robert N. Bellah, "Civil Religion in America in the 70's" quoted in Russell E. Richey, and Donald G. Jones, *American Civil Religion* (New York: Harper and Row, 1974), 21.

14 Ibid., 29.

15 Bellah, "Civil Religion in America in the 70's," 266.

16 Richard Neuhaus, *Time Toward Home* (New York: Seabury, 1975), 207.

17 John Coleman, "Civil Religion and Liberation Theology" quoted in Torres, Sergio and Eagleson (eds.), *Theology in the Americas* (Maryknoll, New York: Orbis Books, 1974), 114.

18 Ibid., 116.

19 Michael Harrington, *The Vast Majority* (New York: Simon and Schuster, 1977), 34.

20 Jűrgen Moltmann, "The Cross and Civil Religion" quoted in Moltmann *et al, Religion and Political Society* (New York: Harper and Row, 1974), 32.

21 Bellah, "Civil Religion in America in the 70's," 257.

22 Ibid., 257.

23 Stephen H. Webb, *American Providence* (New York: Continuum, 2004).

24 Ibid., 4.

25 Ibid., 47ff.

26 Ibid., 22.

27 Ibid., 25.

28 Ibid., 6.

29 Ibid., 7.

30 Ibid., 8.

31 Ibid., 33.

32 Ibid., 39.

33 Ibid., 62.

34 Ibid., 117.

35 Ibid., 126.

36 Ibid., 126.

37 Walter Brueggemann, *The Prophetic Imagination* (Minneapolis: Fortress Press, 2001), 30.

38 Gustavo Gutierrez, *On Job* (Maryknoll, New York: Orbis Books, 1987), 103.

39 Crossan, *God and Empire*, 116.

40 Jon Sobrino, *No Salvation Outside the Poor* (Maryknoll, New York: Orbis Books, 2008), 105.

41 Ibid., 60.

42 Chalmers Johnson, *The Sorrows of Empire* (New York: Henry Holt and Company, 2004), 3.

Chapter Three: SCRIPTURE, THE CHURCH AND EMPIRE

1. The Fellowship, "Faith in Public Life" (Web/internet: 6/25/2009).

2. Richard A. Horsley, *Jesus in Context* (Minneapolis: Fortress Press, 2008), 64.

3. Elisabeth Schussler Fiorenza, *The Power of the Word* (Minneapolis, Fortress Press, 2007), 109.

4. Richard A Horsley, (ed.), *Paul and Empire* (Harrisburg: Trinity Press International, 1997), 1.

5. Horsley, *Jesus in Context*, 70.

6. Ibid., 223.
7. Ibid., 167.
8. Richard A. Horsley, "Jesus and Empire" in *USQR*, Volume 59 (New York, 2005), 63-64.
9. Brian J. Walsh and Sylvia C. Keesmaat, *Colossians Remixed* (Downers Grove: Intervarsity Press, 2004), 69.
10. Richard A. Horsley (ed.), *In the Shadow of Empire* (Louisville: Westminster John Knox Press, 1994), 90.
11. Ibid., 92.
12. William R. Herzog, *Parables as Subversive Speech* (Louisville: Westminster John Knox Press, 1994), 27.
13. Tom Thatcher, *Greater Than Caesar* (Minneapolis: Fortress Press, 2009), 93.
14. Horsley, *Paul and Empire*, 167.
15. Warren Carter, *John and Empire* (New York: T&T Clark, 2008), 289.
16. Fiorenza, *The Power of the Word*, 71.
17. Ibid., 77.
18. Richard A. Horsley, *Covenant Economics* (Louisville: Westminster John Knox Press, 2009), 114.
19. Richard A. Horsley, *Jesus and Empire* (Minneapolis: Fortress Press, 2003), 114.
20. Horsley, *Covenant Economics*, 113.

Chapter Four: RHETORIC AND RESISTANCE

1. James C. Scott, *Domination and the Arts of Resistance* (New Haven: Yale University Press, 1990), 1-44.
2. Richard A. Horsley, *Jesus and Empire* (Minneapolis: Fortress Press, 2003), 113-114.
3. Scott, *Domination and the Arts of Resistance*, 108.
4. Ibid., 118-120.
5. Horsley, *Jesus and Empire*, 134.

6. Ibid., 134.
7. Jon Sobrino, *No Salvation Outside the Poor* (Maryknoll, New York: Orbis Books, 2008), 88.
8. Ibid., 89.
9. Ibid., 91.
10 Ibid., 53.
11 Timothy Parsons, *The Rule of Empire* (New York: Oxford University Press, 2010), 4.
12. Paul King, Kent Maynard, David O. Woodyard, *Risking Liberation: Middle Class Powerlessness* (Atlanta: John Knox Press, 1988).
13 Scott, *Domination and the Arts of Resistance*, 12.
14 Ibid., 4.
15. Michael E. Lee, *Bearing the Weight of Salvation* (New York: The Crossroad Publishing Company, 2009), 67.
16. James Cone, *A Black Theology of Liberation* (Maryknoll, New York: Orbis Books, 1986), 108.
17. Sobrino, *No Salvation Outside the Poor*, 83.
18. Jon Sobrino, *Where Is God?* (Maryknoll, New York: Orbis Books, 2004), viii.
19. Jung Mo Sung, *Desire, Market, and Religion* (London: SCM Press, 2007), 9.
20. Sobrino, *Where Is God?*, xx.
21. Horsley, *Jesus and Empire*, 34.
22. Sobrino, *Where Is God?*, 121 and xxi.
23. Jürgen Moltmann, *The Theology of Hope* (New York: Harper and Row, 1967), 21.
24. Horsley, *Jesus and Empire*, 105
25. Tom Thatcher, *Greater Than Caesar* (Minneapolis: Fortress Press, 2009), 97.
26. Walter Brueggemann, *Prophetic Imagination* (Minneapolis: Fortress Press, 2001), 85.

Chapter Five: WORSHIP IN THE CONTEXT OF EMPIRE

1. Alasdair MacIntyre, quoted in Donald W. Shriver, Jr., *Honest Patriots: Loving a Country Enough to Remember Its Misdeeds* (New York: Oxford University Press, 2008), 163.
2. Kevin J. Madigan and Jon D. Levenson, *Resurrection: The Power of God for Christians and Jews* (New Haven: Yale University Press, 2008), 230.
3. Jűrgen Moltmann, *The Theology of Hope* (New York: Harper and Row, 1965), 158.
4. Ibid., 21.
5. Ibid., 21.
6. Tom F. Driver, *The Magic of Ritual* (San Francisco: Harper Collins, 1991), 13.
7. Melissa Raphael, *The Female Face of God in Auschwitz* (New York: Routledge, 2003), 60.
8. Ibid., 134.
9. Madigan and Levenson, *Resurrection: The Power of God for Christians and Jews*, 23.
10. Driver, *The Magic of Ritual*, 199.
11. Norman K. Gottwald, "Early Israel as an Anti-Imperial Community" quoted in Richard A. Horsley, *In the Shadow of Empire* (Louisville: Westminster John Knox Press, 2008), 22.
12. Walter Brueggeman, *The Prophetic Imagination* (Minneapolis: Fortress Press, 2001), xx.
13. Jűrgen Moltmann, *The Crucified God* (New York: Harper and Row, 1974), 205.
14. Ibid., 205.
15. Dietrich Bonhoeffer, *Letters and Papers from Prison* (New York: Touchstone, 1997), 360.
16. Moltmann, *The Crucified God*, 248.
17. Ignacio Ellacuria, quoted in Kevin F. Burke, *The Ground Beneath the Cross* (Washington, D.C.: Georgetown Press, 2000),

181.

18. Ibid., 26.

19. Ibid., 26.

20. Moltmann, *The Crucified God*, 40.

21. Ibid., 7.

22. Ibid., 136.

23. Tom Thatcher, *Greater Than Caesar* (Minneapolis: Fortress Press, 2009), xix.

Chapter Six: THE ECONOMY AND EMPIRE

1. C. Van Woodward, quoted in Donald W. Shriver, *Honest Patriots: Loving a Country Enough to Remember Its Misdeeds* (New York: Oxford University Press, 2008), 10.

2. Karl Barth, *How to Serve God in a Marxist Land* (New York: Association Press, 1959), 32.

3. Ibid., 50.

4. Ibid., 33.

5. Ibid., 34.

6. Ibid., 49.

7. Walter Brueggemann, *Prophetic Imagination* (Minneapolis: Fortress Press, 2001), 1.

8. Ibid., 1.

9. Ibid., 2.

10. Ibid., 4-5.

11. Ibid., 45.

12. Paul G. King, Kent Maynard, and David O. Woodyard, *Risking Liberation: Middle Class Powerlessness and Social Heroism* (Atlanta: John Knox Press, 1988), 103.

13. Cynthia D. Moe-Lobeda, *Healing a Broken World* (Minneapolis: Fortress Press, 2002), 48.

14. Peter Berger, *The Sacred Canopy* (New York: Doubleday and Co., 1969), 32.

15. Moe-Lobeda, *Healing a Broken World*, 20.
16. Ibid., 22.
17. Ibid., 22.
18. Ibid., 22.
19. Herman Daly and John B. Cobb, Jr., *For the Common Good* (Boston: Beacon Press, 1989), 159.
20. Paul G King, David O. Woodyard, *Liberating Nature* (Atlanta: John Knox Press, 1988), 67.
21. Ibid., 66ff.
22. Ibid., 67.
23. Douglas Meeks, *God the Economist* (Minneapolis: Fortress Press, 1989), 1.
24. Ibid., 158.
25. Ibid., 57.
26. Moe-Lobeda, *Healing a Broken World*, 3.
27. Paul F. Knitter and Chandra Muzaffa, *Subverting Greed: Religious Perspectives on the Global Economy* (Maryknoll, New York: Orbis Books, 2004), 154.
28. Walter Brueggemann, *Cadences of Home* (Louisville: Westminster John Knox, 1997), 29.
29. Shriver, *Honest Patriots: Loving a Country Enough to Remember Its Misdeeds*, 10.
30. Michael Novak, *The Spirit of Democratic Capitalism* (New York: Simon and Schuster, 1982).
31. Jung Mo Sung, *Desire, Market, and Religion* (London: SCM Press, 2007), 39.
32. Ibid., 71.
33. Ibid., 72.
34. Ibid., 95.
35. Ibid., 10.
36. George. Ritzer, *The Globalization of Nothing* (Thousand Oaks, California: Pine George Press, 2004), 72.
37. Moe-Lobeda, *Healing a Broken World*, 4.
38. Sung, *Desire, Market, and Religion*, 26.

39. Kathryn Tanner, *Economy of Grace* (Minneapolis: Fortress Press, 2005), 90.

Chapter Seven: COMMODIFICATION AND COMMUNITY

1. Katheryn Tanner, *Economy of Grace* (Minneapolis: Fortress Press, 2005), 47-48.
2. Ibid., 78.
3. Ibid., 79.
4. Frederic K. Herzog, *Liberation Theology* (New York: The Seabury Press, 1972), 13ff.
5. Boyung Lee, "Re-Creating Our Mother's Dishes" quoted in Rita Nakashima Brock, *et al.* (eds.), *Off the Menu* (Louisville: Westminster John Knox Press, 2007), 298-299.
6. Herzog, *Liberation Theology*, 298.
7. Ibid., 61ff.
8. Musa Dube, quoted in Letty M. Russell, *Just Hospitality* (Louisville: Westminster John Knox Press, 2009), 27-28.
9. Gustavo Gutierrez, quoted in Michael E. Lee, *Bearing the Weight of Salvation* (New York: Crossroad Publishing Company, 2009), 142.
10. Richard A. Horsley, *Jesus and Empire* (Minneapolis: Fortress Press, 2003), 79.
11. Jack Nelson-Pallmeyer, *Saving Christianity From Empire* (New York: Continuum Publishing, 2005), 7.
12. Jürgen Moltmann, *The Theology of Hope* (New York: Harper and Row, 1967), 304.
13. Ibid., 316.
14. Ibid., 324.
15. Ibid., 325.
16. Laurel A. Dykstra, *Set Them Free* (New York: Orbis Books, 2002), 161.
17. Ibid., 148.
18. Ibid., 162.

Chapter Eight: JAMES CONE: A THEOLOGY OF RESISTANCE

1. Stephen D. Moore, *Empire and Apocalypse* (Sheffield, England: Sheffield Phoenix Press, 2006), 61.
2. Emile M. Townes, "Response to 'New Testament and Roman Empire'" (*USQR*, Volume 59, 2005), 76.
3. James H. Cone, *A Black Theology of Liberation* (New York: Orbis Books, 1986), 55.
4. James H. Cone, *For My People* (New York: Orbis Books, 1984), 75.
5. Cone, *A Black Theology of Liberation*, 2.
6. James H. Cone, *Black Theology and Black Power* (New York: The Seabury Press, 1969), 44.
7. Ibid., 44.
8. James H. Cone, *God of the Oppressed* (New York: The Seabury Press, 1975), 164.
9. Ibid., 172.
10. Ibid., 177.
11. Cone, *A Black Theology of Liberation*, 7.
12. Michael Lerner and Cornel West, *Jews and Blacks* (New York: G. P. Putnam's Sons, 1995), 46.
13. Ibid., 47.
14. Ibid., 48.
15. Ibid., 62.
16. Ibid., 163.
17. Cone, *A Black Theology of Liberation*, xiii.
18. Ibid., 24-25.
19. Ibid., 45.
20. Cone, *Black Theology and Black Power*, 10.
21. James H. Cone, *Risks of Faith* (Boston: Beacon Press, 1999), 14.
22. Ibid., 14.
23. Cone, *God of the Oppressed*, 91.
24. Ibid., 93.
25. Cone, *A Black Theology of Liberation*, 9.

26. Ibid., 18.

27. Ibid., 62.

28. Cone, *God of the Oppressed*, 3.

29. Cone, *A Black Theology of Liberation*, 31.

30. James H. Cone, *Speaking the Truth* (Grand Rapids, Michigan: William B. Eerdmans Publishing Company, 1986), 6

31. Tom Driver, *The Magic of Ritual* (San Francisco: HarperCollins, 1991), 3.

32. Ibid., 5.

33. Ibid., 16.

34. Ibid., 16.

35. Ibid., 30.

36. Ibid., 97.

37. Cone, *Risks of Faith*, ix.

38. Ibid., x.

39. Ibid., xiii.

40. Cone, *God of the Oppressed*, 1.

41. Cone, *Speaking the Truth*, 130.

42. James H. Cone, *The Spirituals and the Blues* (New York: The Seabury Press, 1972), 19.

43. Cone, *Risks of Faith*, 13.

44. Ibid., 16.

45. Ibid., 21.

46. Ibid., 26.

47. Ibid., 27.

48. Cone, *God of the Oppressed*, 238.

49. Cone, *A Black Theology of Liberation*, 73-74.

50. Cone, *God of the Oppressed*, 229.

51. Cone, *Risks of Faith*, 14.

Chapter Nine: EPILOGUE

1. Tom Thatcher, *Greater Than Caesar* (Minneapolis: Fortress Press, 2009), 126.
2. Ibid., 139.
3. Ibid., 127.
4. Amos Yong and Samuel Zalanga, "What Empire, Which Multitude?" quoted in Bruce Ellis Benson and Peter Goodwin Heltzel, *Evangelicals and Empire* (Grand Rapids: Brazos Press, 2008), 237.
5. John Micklethwait, and Adrian Wooldridge, *God is Back* (New York: Penguin Press, 2009), 353.
6. Michael Berenbaum, *After Tragedy and Triumph* (New York: Cambridge University Press, 1990), 24.
7. Emil Fackenheim, *God's Presence in History* (New York: Harper and Row, 1970), 6.
8. John D. Caputo, *The Weakness of God* (Indianapolis: Indiana University Press, 2006), 13.
9. Ibid., 14.
10. John D. Caputo, *What Would Jesus Deconstruct?* (Grand Rapids: Baker Academic, 2007), 88.
11. Ibid., 81.
12. Ibid., 82.
13. Thatcher, *Greater Than Caesar*, 88.
14. Ibid., 129.
15. Peter Goodwin Heltzel, *Jesus and Justice* (New Haven: Yale University Press, 2009), 67.
16. Thatcher, *Greater Than Caesar*, 124.
17. Albert Camus, quoted in Mark Lewis Taylor, *The Executed God* (Minneapolis: Fortress Press, 2001), 155.
18. Ibid., 156.
19. Ignacio Ellacuria, quoted in Klein F. Burke and Robert Lassalle-Klein (eds) *Love that Produces Hope* (Collegeville, Minnesota: Liturgical Press, 2006), 198.

20. Walter Brueggeman, *Cadences of Home* (Louisville: Westminster John Knox Press, 1997), 29.

21. Elisabeth Schossler Fiorenza, *The Power of the Word* (Minneapolis: Fortress Press, 2007), 77.

22. Ibid., 78.

23. Brigitte Kahl, *Galatians Re-Imaged* (Minneapolis: Fortress Press, 2010), 261.

24. Jürgen Moltmann, *Sun of Righteousness, ARISE* (Minneapolis: Fortress Press, 2010), 55.

25. George W. Williamson, *Religion on the Wrong Side of the Issue*. Unpublished Manuscript.

INDEX

WORKS
CONSULTED & CITED

THE CONTOURS OF EMPIRE
Chapter One

Albright, Madeline. *The Mighty and the Almighty*. New York: Harper Collins Publishers, 2006.

Bacevich, Andrew J. *The Limits of Power*. New York: Henry Holt and Company, 2008.

Hardt, Michael and Negri, Antonio. *Empire*. Cambridge, Massachusetts: Harvard University Press, 2001.

Hodgson, Godfrey. *The Myth of American Exceptionalism*. New Haven: Yale University Press, 2009.

"Iraq: Setting the Record Straight," The Project for the New American Century, Web page.

Mandelbaum, Michael. *The Case for Goliath*. New York: Public Affairs, 2005.

Meeks, Douglas. *God the Economist*. Minneapolis: Fortress Press, 1989.

Nelson-Pallmeyer, Jack. *Saving Christianity from Empire*. New York: Continuum International Publishing Group, 2005.

Niebuhr, Reinhold. *The Structure of Nations and Empires*. New York: Charles Scribner's Sons, 1959.

Niebuhr, Reinhold. "Awkward Imperialists." *The Atlantic Monthly* May 1930.

Parsons, Timothy H. *The Rule of Empires: Those Who Built Them, Those Who Endured Them, and Why They Always Fail*. New York: Oxford University Press, 2010.

Robinson, Randall. *The Debt: What America Owes to Blacks*. New York: Penguin Books, 2000.

"Rebuilding America's Defenses." The Project for the New
American Century, Web page.

Shriver, Donald W., Jr. *Honest Patriots: Loving a Country Enough
to Remember Its Misdeeds*. New York: Oxford University Press,
2008.

Winthrop, John. "A Model of Christian Charity" in Cherry, Conrad.
God's New Israel. Englewood Cliffs, New Jersey: Prentice-Hall.

EMPIRE AND TRANSCENDENCE
Chapter Two

Bellah, Robert N. "Civil Religion in America" in Richey, Russell E.
and Jones, Donald G. *American Civil Religion*. New York:
Harper and Row. 1974.

Bellah, Robert N. "Civil Religion in America in the 70's" quoted in
Richey, Russell E. and Jones, Donald G. *American Civil Religion*.
New York: Harper and Row. 1974.

Brueggemann, Walter. *Prophetic Imagination*. Minneapolis:
Fortress Press, 2001.

Coleman, John. "Civil Religion and Liberation Theology" quoted
in Torres, Sergio and Eagleson (eds.), *Theology in the Americas*.
Maryknoll, New York: Orbis Books, 1974.

Crossan, John Dominic. *God and Empire*. San Francisco: Harper
Collins, 2007.

Griffin, David Ray, et al. *The American Empire and the Commonwealth
of God*. Louisville: Westminster John Knox, 2007.

Gutierrez, Gustavo. *On Job*. Maryknoll, New York: Orbis Books,
1987.

Harrington, Michael. *The Vast Majority*. New York: Simon and
Schuster, 1977.

Hodgson, Godfrey. *The Myth of American Exceptionalism*. New
Haven: Yale University Press, 2009.

Johnson, Chalmers. *The Sorrows of Empire*. New York: Henry Holt and Company, 2004.

Keller, Catherine. "Omnipotence and Preemption" quoted in Griffin, David Ray et al. *The American Empire and the Commonwealth of God*. Louisville: Westminster John Knox Press, 2006.

Keller, Catherine. *God and Power*. Minneapolis: Fortress Press, 2005.

King, Paul G. and Woodyard, David O. *Liberating Nature*. Cleveland: The Pilgrim Press, 1999.

Moltmann, Jürgen. "The Cross and Civil Religion" quoted in Moltmann et al. *Religion and Political Society*. New York: Harper and Row, 1974.

Neuhaus, Richard. *Time Toward Home*. New York: Seabury, 1975.

Rieger, Joerg. "Christian Theology and Empires" in Pui-lan, Kwok et al. *Empire and the Christian Tradition*. Minneapolis: Fortress Press, 2007.

Ritzer, George. *The Globalization of Nothing*. Thousand Oaks, California: Pine George Press, 2003.

Sobrino, Jon. *No Salvation Outside the Poor*. Maryknoll, New York: Orbis Books, 2008.

Webb, Stephen H. *American Providence*. New York: Continuum, 2004.

SCRIPTURE, THE CHURCH, AND EMPIRE
Chapter Three

Carter, Warren. *John and Empire*. New York: T&T Clark, 2008.

Fiorenza, Elisabeth Schussler. *The Power of the Word*. Minneapolis: Fortress Press, 2007.

Herzog, William R. *Parables as Subversive Speech*. Louisville: Westminster John Knox Press, 1994.

Horsley, Richard A. *Jesus in Context*. Minneapolis: Fortress Press, 2008.

Horsley, Richard A. (ed.). *Paul and Empire*. Harrisburg: Trinity Press International, 1997.

Horsley, Richard A. (ed.). *In the Shadow of Empire*. Louisville: Westminster John Knox Press, 1994.

Horsley, Richard A. *Covenant Economics*. Louisville: Westminster John Knox Press, 2009.

Horsley, Richard A. *Jesus and Empire*. Minneapolis: Fortress Press, 2003.

Horsley, Richard A. "Jesus and Empire" in *USQR*, Volume 59. New York: 2005.

Thatcher, Tom. *Greater Than Caesar*. Minneapolis: Fortress Press, 2009.

Walsh, Brian J. and Keesmaat, Sylvia C. *Colossians Remixed*. Downers Grove: Intervarsity Press, 2004.

Web/internet. "Faith in Public Life" 6/25/2009.

RETORIC AND RESISTANCE
Chapter Four

Brueggemann, Walter. *Prophetic Imagination*. Minneapolis: Fortress Press, 2001.

Cone, James. *A Black Theology of Liberation*. Maryknoll, New York: Orbis Books, 1986.

Horsley, Richard A. *Jesus and Empire*. Minneapolis: Fortress press, 2003.

King, Paul, Maynard, Kent, Woodyard, David O. *Risking Liberation: Middle Class Powerlessness*. Atlanta: John Knox Press, 1988.

Lee, Michael E. *Bearing the Weight of Salvation*. New York: The Crossroad Publishing Company, 2009.

Moltmann, Jürgen. *The Theology of Hope*. New York: Harper and Row, 1967.

Parsons, Timothy, *The Rule of Empires*. New York: Oxford

University Press, 2010.

Scott, James C. *Domination and the Arts of Resistance*. New Haven: Yale University Press, 1990.

Sobrino, Jon. *No Salvation Outside the Poor*. Maryknoll, New York: Orbis Books, 2008.

Sobrino, Jon. *Where Is God?* Maryknoll, New York: Orbis Books, 2004.

Sung, Jung Mo. *Desire, Market, and Religion*. London: SCM Press, 2007.

Thatcher, Tom. *Greater Than Caesar*. Minneapolis: Fortress Press, 2009.

WORSHIP IN THE CONTEXT OF EMPIRE
Chapter Five

Bonhoeffer, Dietrich. *Letters and Papers from Prison*. New York: Touchstone, 1997.

Brueggemann, Walter. *The Prophetic Imagination*. Minneapolis: Fortress Press, 2001.

Burke, Kevin F. (S.J.). *The Ground Beneath the Cross*. Washington, D.C.: Georgetown Press, 2000.

Driver, Tom F. *The Magic of Ritual*. San Francisco: Harper Collins, 1991.

Gottwald, Norman K. "Early Israel as an Anti-Imperial Community" quoted in Horsley, Richard A. *In the Shadow of Empire*. Louisville: Westminster John Knox Press, 2008.

Madigan, Kevin J. and Levenson, Jon D. *Resurrection: The Power of God for Christians and Jews*. New Haven: Yale University Press, 2008.

Moltmann, Jürgen. *The Crucified God*. New York: Harper and Row, 1974.

Moltmann, Jürgen. *The Theology of Hope*. New York: Harper and Row, 1965.

Raphael, Melissa. *The Female Face of God in Auschwitz*. New York: Routledge, 2003.

Shriver, Donald W., Jr. *Honest Patriots: Loving a Country Enough to Remember Its Misdeeds*. New York: Oxford University Press, 2008.

Thatcher, Tom. *Greater Than Caesar*. Minneapolis: Fortress Press, 2009.

THE ECONOMY AND EMPIRE
Chapter Six

Barth, Karl. *How to Serve God in a Marxist Land*. New York: Association Press, 1959.

Berger, Peter. *The Sacred Canopy*. New York: Doubleday and Co., 1969.

Brueggemann, Walter. *Prophetic Imagination*. Minneapolis: Fortress Press, 2001.

Brueggemann, Walter. *Cadences of Home*. Louisville: Westminster John Knox, 1997.

Cobb, John Jr. and Daly, Herman. *For the Common Good*. Boston: Beacon Press, 1989.

Daly, Herman and John B. Cobb, Jr. *For the Common Good*. Boston: Beacon Press, 1989.

King, Paul G., Maynard, Kent, Woodyard, David O. *Risking Liberation: Middle Class Powerlessness and Social Heroism*. Atlanta: John Knox Press, 1988.

King, Paul G. and Woodyard, David O. *Liberating Nature*. Atlanta: John Knox Press, 1988.

Knitter, Paul F and Muzaffar, Chandra. *Subverting Greed: Religious Perspectives on the Global Economy*. Maryknoll, New York: Orbis Books, 2004.

Meeks, Douglas. *God the Economist*. Minneapolis: Fortress Press, 1989.

Moe-Lobeda, Cynthia D. *Healing a Broken World*. Minneapolis: Fortress Press, 2002.

Novak, Michael. *The Spirit of Democratic Capitalism*. New York: Simon and Schuster, 1982.

Ritzer, George. *The Globalization of Nothing*. Thousand Oaks, California: Pine George Press, 2004.

Shriver, Donald W., Jr. *Honest Patriots: Loving a Country Enough to Remember Its Misdeeds*. New York: Oxford University Press, 2008.

Sung, Jung Mo. *Desire, Market, and Religion*. London: SCM Press, 2007.

Tanner, Kathryn. *Economy of Grace*. Minneapolis: Fortress Press, 2005.

COMMODIFICATION AND COMMUNITY
Chapter Seven

Brock, Rita Nakashima *et al*. (eds.) *Off the Menu*. Louisville: Westminster John Knox Press, 2007.

Dykstra, Laurel A. *Set Them Free*. New York: Orbis Books, 2002.

Herzog, Frederic K. *Liberation Theology*. New York: The Seabury Press, 1972.

Horsley, Richard A. *Jesus and Empire*. Minneapolis: Fortress Press, 2003.

Lee, Michael E. *Bearing the Weight of Salvation*. New York: Crossroad Publishing Company, 2009.

Mandelbaum, Michael. *The Case For Goliath*. New York: Public Affairs, 2005.

Moltmann, Jürgen. *The Theology of Hope*. New York: Harper and Row, 1967.

Nelson-Pallmeyer, Jack. *Saving Christianity From Empire*. New York: Continuum Publishing, 2005.

Russell, Letty M. *Just Hospitality*. Louisville: Westminster John

Knox Press, 2009.

Tanner, Kathryn. *Economy of Grace*. Minneapolis: Fortress Press, 2005.

JAMES CONE: A THEOLOGY OF RESISTANCE
Chapter Eight

Cone, James H. *A Black Theology of Liberation*. New York: Orbis Books, 1986.

Black Theology and Black Power. New York: The Seabury Press, 1969.

For My People. New York: Orbis Books, 1984.

God of the Oppressed. New York: The Seabury Press, 1975.

Risks of Faith. Boston: Beacon Press, 1999.

Speaking the Truth. Grand Rapids, Michigan: William B. Eerdmans Publishing Company, 1986.

The Spirituals and the Blues. New York: The Seabury Press, 1972.

Driver, Tom. *The Magic of Ritual*. San Francisco: HarperCollins, 1991.

Lerner, Michael and West, Cornel. *Jews and Blacks*. New York: G. P. Putnam's Sons, 1995.

Moore, Stephen D. *Empire and Apocalypse*. Sheffield, England: Sheffield Phoenix Press, 2006.

Townes, Emile M. "Response to 'New Testament and Roman Empire'." *USQR*, Volume 59, 2005.

EPILOGUE
Chapter Nine

Berenbaum, Michael, *After Tragedy and Triumph*. New York: Cambridge University Press, 1990.

Brueggemann, Walter. *Cadences of Home*. Louisville: Westminster John Knox Press, 1997.

Burke, Kevin F. and Lassalle-Klein, Robert (eds). *Love that Produces Hope.* Collegeville, Minnesota: Liturgical Press, 2006.

Camus, Albert, quoted in Taylor, Mark Lewis. *The Executed God.* Minneapolis: Fortress Press, 2001.

Caputo, John D. *The Weakness of God.* Indianapolis: Indiana University Press, 2006.

Caputo, John D. *What Would Jesus Deconstruct?* Grand Rapids: Baker Academic, 2007.

Fackenheim, Emil. *God's Presence in History.* New York: Harper and Row, 1970.

Fiorenza, Elisabeth Schossler, *The Power of the Word.* Minneapolis: Fortress Press, 2007.

Heltzel, Peter Goodwin. *Jesus and Justice.* New Haven: Yale University Press, 2009.

Kahl, Brigitte. *Galatians Re-Imaged.* Minneapolis: Fortress Press, 2010.

Micklethwait, John and Wooldridge, Adrian. *God is Back.* New York: Penguin Press, 2009.

Moltmann, Jürgen. *Sun of Righteousness, ARISE.* Minneapolis: Fortress Press, 2010.

Taylor, Mark Lewis. *The Executed God.* Minneapolis: Fortress Press, 2001.

Thatcher, Tom. *Greater Than Caesar.* Minneapolis: Fortress Press, 2009.

Williamson, George W. *Religion on the Wrong Side of the Issue.* Unpublished Manuscript.

Yong, Amos and Zalanga, Samuel. "What Empire, Which Multitude?" quoted in Benson, Bruce Ellis and Heltzel, Peter Goodwin (eds), *Evangelicals and Empire.* Grand Rapids: Brazos Press, 2008.

B O O K S

O is a symbol of the world, of oneness and unity. In different cultures it also means the "eye," symbolizing knowledge and insight. We aim to publish books that are accessible, constructive and that challenge accepted opinion, both that of academia and the "moral majority."

Our books are available in all good English language bookstores worldwide. If you don't see the book on the shelves ask the bookstore to order it for you, quoting the ISBN number and title. Alternatively you can order online (all major online retail sites carry our titles) or contact the distributor in the relevant country, listed on the copyright page.

See our website **www.o-books.net** for a full list of over 500 titles, growing by 100 a year.

And tune in to myspiritradio.com for our book review radio show, hosted by June-Elleni Laine, where you can listen to the authors discussing their books.